Neighborhood in Motion
Stadtquartier in Bewegung

Neighborhood in Motion
Stadtquartier in Bewegung

Konrad Otto-Zimmermann
Yeonhee Park (Eds./Hg.)

One Neighborhood, One Month, No Cars.
An Urban Experiment Transforming Spaces, Mindset, and Lifestyle
Ein Stadtquartier, ein Monat, autofrei.
Ein städtisches Experiment verändert Stadtraum, Denkart und Lebensstil

jovis

Contents
Inhalt

1 Portrait of a Unique Experiment
Porträt eines einzigartigen Experiments

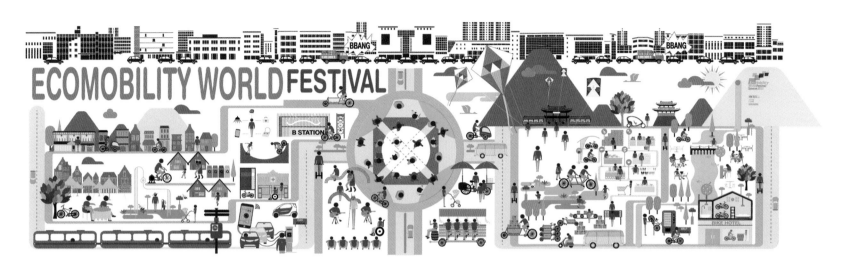

This is the story of a unique project.

The Mayor of Suwon had the idea to prepare citizens for urban life in an era of dwindling fossil resources and low-carbon energy supply.

It was conceived as a mise en scène of future car-free mobility in one neighborhood.

The festival format was chosen to make the experience fun for young and old, resident and visitors.

It was planned with the intent to initialize a process of cautious urban renewal in the Haenggung-dong neighborhood.

The effect was surprising: residents saw the benefit not only in changing to mobility habits that have a positive environmental impact, but even more, they experienced a rediscovery of community, the revival of social contacts. This was initially instigated through controversial debates about the real meaning of a car-free month, and then further enabled through the public space freed from cars.

The festival project turned into a fascinating social experiment, the spirit of which, residents want to preserve.

Dies ist die Geschichte eines einzigartigen Projekts.

Die Idee des Bürgermeisters von Suwon war es, die Bürger auf ein Stadtleben im Zeitalter schwindender Erdölvorräte und CO_2-armer Energieversorgung vorzubereiten.

Konzipiert war es als eine Inszenierung zukünftiger autofreier Mobilität in einem Stadtquartier.

Als Festival wurde es veranstaltet, damit es ein Spaß für Jung und Alt, für Bewohner und Besucher würde.

Geplant wurde es mit der Absicht, mit dem Festival eine behutsame Stadterneuerung des Haenggung-dong-Quartiers einzuleiten.

Der Verlauf war überraschend: Die Bewohner sahen den Nutzen nicht allein in veränderten Mobilitätsgewohnheiten mit positiven Umwelteffekten, sondern vor allem in der Wiederentdeckung der Nachbarschaft, dem Wiederaufleben sozialer Kontakte – zunächst angestoßen durch kontroverse Debatten um den autofreien Monat, sodann ermöglicht durch den von Autos befreiten öffentlichen Raum.

Aus einem Festivalprojekt wurde ein soziales Experiment. Die meisten Bewohner möchten diese Erfahrung nicht mehr missen.

Experience How it Will Be in the Future

" I have been living in Haenggung-dong for sixty-four years.
After I retired, I started to use bicycles; that was twenty years ago. I made it a habit to use bicycles. I do it for my health rather than for the environment. For short distances up to thirty minutes I take a bike, for longer distances I use subways and buses.
The fossil fuels will be exhausted someday. The EcoMobility Festival is very important because we can experience how it will be in the future. It is a simulation process. The festival also helps residents to cooperate with each other. Hence, it is very good for community union. Even though many residents disagreed with the idea at first, they now gather more often in public. We need to reduce the dependency on cars. It is important to do that, so we should bear the discomfort. But we cannot force the people to abandon their cars, as we are all very used to driving our vehicles. Furthermore, after Korea became rich in the nineteen-seventies, the car became a symbol of having money. People worry that others will look down on them if they stop using cars. So one problem is the social stereotype about cars and the social pressure associated with it. "

Seong Woo Lee,
President of the Elderly Community

The Vision that has become true.

Die Vision, die wahr wurde.

„ Ich lebe seit 64 Jahren in Haeng-gung-dong.
Nach meiner Pensionierung begann ich, Fahrrad zu fahren, das war vor 20 Jahren. Radfahren wurde mir zur Gewohnheit. Ich tue es mehr für meine Gesundheit als für die Umwelt. Für kurze Fahrten bis zu 30 Minuten nehme ich das Fahrrad, für weitere Fahrten benutze ich U-Bahn und Busse.
Die fossilen Brennstoffe werden eines Tages erschöpft sein. Das EcoMobility-Festival ist sehr wichtig, weil wir erfahren können, wie es in der Zukunft sein wird. Es ist ein Simulationsprozess. Das Festival hilft den Bewohnern auch, zusammenzu-arbeiten. Daher ist es sehr gut für die soziale Gemeinschaft. Obwohl viele Bewohner zuerst gegen die Idee waren, kommen sie nun öfters im öffentlichen Raum zusammen.
Wir müssen die Abhängigkeit vom Auto vermindern. Es ist wichtig, dies zu tun; also sollten wir die Unbe-quemlichkeit ertragen. Aber wir können die Leute nicht zwingen, ihre Autos aufzugeben, da wir alle es sehr gewohnt sind, sie zu nutzen. Außerdem wurde das Auto in den 1970er Jahren zum Statussymbol, als Korea reich wurde. Die Leute haben Sorge, dass andere auf sie herabblicken, wenn sie aufhören, Auto zu fahren. Ein Problem ist also das soziale Klischee und der damit verbundene soziale Druck. **„**

Seong Woo Lee,
Präsident der Seniorengemeinschaft

From Idea to Commitment
Von der Idee zum Versprechen

Origin of the Idea

❝ As a boy, I loved my push scooter and later my bicycle. I envied others who had a pedal car. I was impressed by the way human-powered vehicles could bring comfort and speed, carry pets and other loads. The son of a local newspaper editor and a city councilor, it was a fascination with the concepts of town and local community that made me study architecture and urban planning, as well as public administration.

In the late nineteen-seventies, I met the Munich-based architect Hermann Grub. I was deeply impressed by the 'action art' he staged to surprise the public, raise awareness, and provoke discussion*). The image of a street space or square converted overnight never left my mind. The vision of a car-free, ecomobile city sprouted in my mind.

In the nineteen-eighties, I managed the German 'Bicycle-friendly City' project at the German Federal Environmental Agency. After seven years of research, planning, and roundtables, a few bicycle lanes were marked in the streets, cycling promotion centers were in operation, and the modal share of cycling had indeed doubled in each participating city. But we were far from images of 'cities of cyclists.'

My patience has since shrunk, and it is with an increasing sense of urgency that I see the need to move away from the current pattern of automobile-based urban mobility. If we want to produce images of car-free transport and an ecomobile lifestyle in real cities of the world, we cannot wait for model cities to emerge. We must work with a temporary mise en scène in a real city, with real citizens, in real time, using a methodology that I call CityScene. We must stage it playfully and pleasantly as a festival. The idea of the EcoMobility World Festival with its CityScene approach was born. ❞

Konrad Otto-Zimmermann

*) Esser, Stefan: *Grub + Lejeune. Nachhaltige Stadtentwicklung—Konzepte, Aktionen, Projekte.* München, o. J.

Ursprung der Idee

❞ Als Junge liebte ich meinen Ballonroller und später mein Fahrrad. Ich beneidete andere, die ein Tretauto besaßen. Ich war beeindruckt davon, wie bequem und schnell menschenbewegte Fahrzeuge waren und wie sie Haustiere und Gepäck befördern konnten. Es war die Faszination von Stadt und Kommune, die mich als Sohn eines Lokalredakteurs und einer Stadträtin Architektur und Stadtplanung sowie Verwaltungswissenschaften studieren ließ. Ende der 1970er Jahre begegnete ich dem Münchner Architekten Hermann Grub. Ich war tief beeindruckt von der ‚Aktionskunst‘, mit der er die Öffentlichkeit überraschte, Bewusstsein schaffte und Diskussionen provozierte.*) Das Bild eines über Nacht verwandelten Straßenraumes oder Platzes ließ mich nicht wieder los. Die Vision einer autofreien, ökomobilen Stadt keimte in mir.

In den 1980ern leitete ich das deutsche Modellvorhaben ‚Fahrradfreundliche Stadt‘ beim Umweltbundesamt. Nach sieben Jahren Forschung, Planung und Expertenrunden gab es zwar markierte Fahrradwege, Fahrradbüros waren eingerichtet und der Fahrradverkehrsanteil hatte sich in jeder teilnehmenden Stadt verdoppelt. Von ‚Radfahrer-Städten‘ waren wir jedoch noch weit entfernt.

Meine Geduld ist ob der Dringlichkeit, mit der wir uns vom derzeitigen Muster autobasierter städtischer Mobilität abkehren müssen, aber geschrumpft. Wenn wir Bilder von autofreiem Stadtverkehr und ökomobilem Lebensstil in existierenden Städten der Welt produzieren wollen, können wir nicht das Entstehen von Modellstädten abwarten. Wir müssen mit kurzzeitigen Inszenierungen arbeiten, in einer echten Stadt, mit echten Bürgern und in Echtzeit – eine Methode, die ich CityScene nenne. Wir müssen dies spielerisch und freundlich, in Form eines Festivals, tun. Damit war die Idee des EcoMobility World Festivals mit seinem CityScene-Ansatz geboren. ❝

Konrad Otto-Zimmermann

*) Esser, Stefan: *Grub + Lejeune. Nachhaltige Stadtentwicklung – Konzepte, Aktionen, Projekte.* München, o. J.

City Sought, Suwon Found

It would take political courage, assertiveness, and perseverance to organize an EcoMobility World Festival. This requires working with residents, so that they would live car-free for a month and transform their neighborhood into an ecomobile living space. It was with this in mind that Konrad Otto-Zimmermann, then Secretary General of the world cities association ICLEI, explained his project idea to every Mayor that he met, waiting for one of his conversation partners to say: "We can do this."

He invited UN-HABITAT to become a partner to the festival and prepared a joint call for a project city by ICLEI and UN-HABITAT. The announcement was scheduled for the first EcoMobility World Congress in October 2011 in the South Korean city of Changwon. On the eve of the congress, Mayor Tae-young Yeom of Suwon arrived and asked Otto-Zimmermann to explain the project once more. He decided on the spot that Suwon would host the festival. UN-HABITAT Executive Director Dr. Joan Clos and Konrad Otto-Zimmermann presented the project at the congress, and Mayor Yeom approached the podium to announce that the festival would be held in Suwon in 2013.

The world learned about the Suwon festival project through a media release on 23 October 2011. During the following weeks the roles crystallized:
Suwon City, ICLEI, and UN-HABITAT would work together as festival Partners;
Suwon City and ICLEI would function as organizers;
ICLEI and UN-HABITAT would act as presenters of the festival.
 ICLEI secured support from Dr. Florian Lennert (InnoZ Berlin) und Gil Peñalosa (8-80 Cities) as international advisors.

Stadt gesucht, Suwon gefunden

Ein EcoMobility World Festival zu veranstalten, das heißt, mit den Bewohnern eines Stadtquartiers zu arbeiten, damit sie einen Monat lang autofrei leben, und dieses Stadtquartier zeitweise zu einem ökomobilen Lebensraum umzugestalten. Das erfordert politischen Mut, Durchsetzungskraft und Durchhaltevermögen. Deshalb erzählte Konrad Otto-Zimmermann, seinerzeit Generalsekretär des Weltstädteverbandes ICLEI, jedem Bürgermeister, den er traf, von seiner Projektidee und wartete, bis ein Gesprächspartner sagen würde: „Das machen wir!".

Um die Dinge voranzutreiben, lud er die Weltsiedlungsorganisation UN-HABITAT ein, Partner des Festivalprojekts zu werden, und bereitete einen gemeinsamen Aufruf von ICLEI und UN-HABITAT zur Suche nach einer Projektstadt vor. Die Bekanntgabe war für den ersten EcoMobility-Weltkongress im Oktober 2011 in der südkoreanischen Stadt Changwon vorgesehen. Am Vorabend der Bekanntgabe reiste der Bürgermeister der Stadt Suwon, Tae-young Yeom, mit einer städtischen Delegation an, ließ Otto-Zimmermann das Festivalprojekt erläutern und entschied an Ort und Stelle, dass die Stadt Suwon das Festival veranstalten werde. Im Plenum des Kongresses präsentierten UN-HABITAT-Exekutivdirektor Dr. Joan Clos und Konrad Otto-Zimmermann das Projekt. Dann schritt Bürgermeister Yeom ans Podium und kündigte das Festival in Suwon für das Jahr 2013 an.

Am 23. Oktober 2011 erfuhr die Welt durch eine Pressemitteilung ICLEIs vom Festivalprojekt in Suwon. In den Folgewochen wurden die Rollen fixiert:
Stadt Suwon, ICLEI und UN-HABITAT als Festival-Partner;
Stadt Suwon und ICLEI als Organisatoren;
ICLEI und UN-HABITAT würden das Festival präsentieren.
ICLEI gewann die Unterstützung durch Dr. Florian Lennert (InnoZ Berlin) und Gil Peñalosa (8-80 Cities) als internationale Berater.

EcoMobility

The term EcoMobility includes: "walking—cycling—wheeling—'passenging'—carsharing." The concept establishes a clear ranking among the various modes of urban transport.

EcoMobility

schließt ein: Gehen – Radfahren – Handwagen nutzen – ÖPNV nutzen – Carsharing. Das Konzept der Öko-mobilität etabliert eine klare Prioritätenreihung bei der Nutzung städtischer Verkehrsarten.

◁
Once Mayor Yeom returned to Suwon from Changwon, he convened meetings with politicians, municipal officials, and local stakeholders to garner support for the ambitious undertaking.
Sobald Bürgermeister Yeom von Changwon nach Suwon zurückgekehrt war, berief er Sitzungen mit Politikern, städtischen Mitarbeitern und örtlichen Interessensgruppen ein, um sich Unterstützung für das ehrgeizige Unterfangen zu sichern.

EcoMobility in Korean

Finding an appropriate term was a challenge. A corresponding word in Korean does not exist. After extensive consultations and careful consideration, Suwon City chose the Korean term "Sengtae Gyotong"—eco-transport. This, however, does not quite correspond to the meaning of Eco"Mobility," which expresses the subjective state of being mobile. The term "mobility" is people-centered, while "transport" makes the person or good carried an object. Therefore, EcoMobility needed to be explained again and again.

EcoMobility auf Koreanisch

Die koreanische Sprache hält keinen entsprechenden Begriff bereit. Nach Beratungen und reiflicher Überlegung wählte die Stadt Suwon den Begriff „Sengtae Gyotong " – Öko-Transport. Dieser entspricht jedoch nicht ganz der Bedeutung von Öko-„Mobilität", was den subjektiven Zustand, mobil zu sein, beschreibt. Der Ausdruck „Mobilität" setzt den Menschen in den Mittelpunkt, während „Transport" den beförderten Menschen oder die Ware zum Objekt macht. EcoMobility musste daher wieder und wieder erklärt werden.

Organizing an EcoMobility World Festival was anything but routine. The initiators needed to communicate a festival project that was to be a globally unique happening.

First, the English technical term "EcoMobility"—coined by Konrad Otto-Zimmermann and introduced by ICLEI only in 2007—was not common in Korea. A Korean term needed to be introduced and defined.

Secondly, though festivals are well known and appreciated in Korea, when Koreans hear "festival," they think of cultural, music, garden, or flower festivals. The Korean partners had to be familiarized with the idea that a festival could just as easily center on urban mobility and lifestyle.

Thirdly, this festival was not an event organized for citizen and visitors to watch and enjoy—it was a mise en scène, where residents' everyday life was to be experienced in a car-free context.

Ein EcoMobility World Festival zu organisieren, war fern von jeglicher Routine. Die Initiatoren mussten ein Festivalprojekt kommunizieren, welches ein weltweit einmaliges Happening sein würde.

Erstens war der englische Fachbegriff „EcoMobility", geprägt von Konrad Otto-Zimmermann und von ICLEI erst im Jahr 2007 eingeführt, natürlich in Korea nicht gebräuchlich. Ein koreanischer Begriff musste eingeführt und definiert werden.

Zweitens sind Festivals in Korea zwar bekannt und geschätzt, aber wenn Koreaner „Festival" hören, denken sie an Kultur-, Musik-, Garten- oder Blumenfestivals. Die koreanischen Partner mussten mit dem Gedanken vertraut gemacht werden, dass es auch ein Festival rund um städtische Mobilität und Lebensstil geben kann.

Drittens sollten bei diesem Festival Bürger und Besucher nicht einfach zuschauen und sich erfreuen – es war eine Inszenierung, um Bewohner das tägliche Leben unter den Bedingungen eines autofreien Stadtquartiers erleben zu lassen.

Mayor
Bürgermeister

Tae-young Yeom:

- Elected as mayor of Suwon City, South Korea in 2010. Dared to engage in the first ever EcoMobility World Festival.
- An environmental activist for over fifteen years. Working with local NGOs, succeeded in fighting the concrete covering of the "Suwon Stream" watercourse and initiated the river restoration project.
- Since HABITAT II in Istanbul 1996, deeply interested in Local Agenda 21. Established Suwon Agenda 21, as well as Green Gyeonggi (Province) 21. Instrumental in organizing the Korean national LA21 network. Secretary-General of the Korean Council of Local Agenda 21 and Secretary of the Korean Presidential Committee on Sustainable Development.
- Member of the Global Executive Committee and East Asia Regional Executive Committee of ICLEI.

Tae-young Yeom:

- Als Bürgermeister der Stadt Suwon gewählt im Jahr 2010. Wagte es, sich auf das weltweit erste Eco-Mobility World Festival einzulassen.
- Umweltaktivist seit über 15 Jahren. Arbeitet mit örtlichen Verbänden, hatte Erfolg im Kampf gegen die Betonabdeckung des Suwon Stream und initiierte das Projekt zur Flusswiederherstellung.
- Seit HABITAT II in Istanbul 1996 stark interessiert an der Lokalen Agenda 21. Etablierte die „Suwon Agenda 21" sowie das Projekt „Grüne Provinz Gyeonggi 21". War beteiligt an der Organisation des koreanischen landesweiten LA21-Netzwerks. Generalsekretär des Koreanischen Rates für Lokale Agenda 21. Sekretär des Koreanischen Präsidialkomitees für Nachhaltige Entwicklung.
- Mitglied des Weltvorstandes und des Ostasienvorstandes von ICLEI.

" What an amazing person. An environmentalist by conviction. A politician by nature. A daring Mayor. A strategist. A bundle of energy. A people person. Moreover, a citizen-oriented, down-to-earth man who likes people. After the triumph of the festival, I was convinced: the man who has mobilized hundreds of city officials and thousands of supporters and volunteers to pull off the ambitious EcoMobility World Festival, that man can move mountains. He can successfully accomplish any other ambitious project for the benefits of the citizens of Suwon. "

Konrad Otto-Zimmermann

" Was für eine erstaunliche Person. Ein Umweltschützer aus Überzeugung. Ein Politiker von Natur. Ein wagemutiger Bürgermeister. Ein Stratege. Ein Energiebündel. Ein geselliger Mensch. Außerdem ein bürgerorientierter, bodenständiger Mann, der Menschen liebt. Nach dem Meisterstück des Festivals war ich überzeugt: Derjenige, der Hunderte von städtischen Mitarbeitern und Tausende von Unterstützern und Freiwilligen mobilisiert hat , das ehrgeizige Projekt des EcoMobility World Festivals zustande zu bringen, derjenige kann Berge versetzen. Derjenige kann jegliches andere ehrgeizige Projekt für den Nutzen der Bürger von Suwon zuwege bringen. "

Konrad Otto-Zimmermann

Creative Director
Kreativdirektor

Konrad Otto-Zimmermann

- Born 1951 in Detmold, Germany. Already as child a keen user of push scooters, pedal cars, and bicycles.
- Studied architecture and urban planning at the Technical University of Hannover, Germany, as well as Public Administration at the German University of Administrative Sciences Speyer. As a student, active in the citizen initiatives movement.
- Created and promoted the brand "Öffi" ("pubby") for the ponderous German word "Öffentlicher Personennahverkehr" (local public transport), coined the term "Umweltverbund" to name the entirety of alternatives to the private automobiles and created the international brand "EcoMobility" as a single term to encapsulate walking, cycling, wheeling, passenging, and carsharing.
- Managed the German "Bicycle-friendly City" model project during the nineteen-eighties—an experience that shaped the idea of the EcoMobility World Festival.
- Had the idea of a mise en scène of a car-free, ecomobile neighborhood. As Secretary General of ICLEI, initiated and led the EcoMobility World Festival 2013 in Suwon, South Korea, as its Creative Director.
- Today, as Creative Director at The Urban Idea based in Freiburg, Germany, he continues to develop CityScene projects, working towards new urban futures.

Konrad Otto-Zimmermann

- Geboren 1951 in Detmold. Schon als Kind ein begeisterter Nutzer von Rollern, Tretautos und Fahrrädern.
- Studierte Architektur und Stadtplanung an der Technischen Universität Hannover sowie Verwaltungswissenschaften an der Hochschule für Verwaltungswissenschaften Speyer. Während der Studentenzeit aktiv in der Bürgerinitiativen-Bewegung.
- Schuf und verbreitete das Wort „Öffi" für den gestelzten deutschen Begriff „öffentlicher Personennahverkehr", prägte den Begriff „Umweltverbund" für die Gesamtheit der Alternativen zum Privatauto und prägte für den internationalen Diskurs das Wort „EcoMobility", um Gehen, Radfahren, das Benutzen jeglicher Zieh- und Schiebewagen, die Nutzung von Öffis sowie Carsharing mit einem einzelnen Begriff zu benennen.
- Leitete während der 80er Jahre das deutsche Modellvorhaben „Fahrradfreundliche Stadt", eine Erfahrung, die die Idee des EcoMobility-Weltfestivals prägte.
- Hatte die Idee zur Inszenierung eines autofreien, ökomobilen Stadtquartiers. Initiierte das EcoMobility World Festival 2013 in Suwon, Südkorea und leitete es als Kreativdirektor.
- Heute entwickelt er als Kreativdirektor bei The Urban Idea, Freiburg, weitere CityScene-Projekte und arbeitet an neuen Zukünften für unsere Städte.

Vibrant Suwon

Suwon, with its 1.2 million inhabitants, is the capital city of Gyeonggi, which is the largest province in South Korea and surrounds the national capital, Seoul. Suwon is an educational center with eleven universities, an industrial hub, and the seat of Samsung Electronics' research and development center and headquarters. Hwaseong Fortress, a UNESCO World Heritage site and the only remaining completely walled city in South Korea, also makes the city a popular tourist destination.

Beyond its historic center, a visiting urbanist would perceive Suwon as a typical Korean city with modern residential quarters and, densely populated high-rise buildings. A transport planner might see Suwon as a city of cars and buses.

The political leadership of Suwon has been eager to embrace environmental initiatives and make the city an internationally recognized player. In 2005, Suwon joined ICLEI, the world's largest network of local governments dedicated to sustainable development. Since then, it has hosted international environmental conferences and the current Mayor, Tae-young Yeom, serves on ICLEI's governing bodies.

Suwon aims at nothing more modest than becoming Korea's eco-capital.

Selection of a Neighborhood

How does one create an ecomobile city? Removing cars from an entire city for a full month appeared to be unrealistic. Working with the residents of a single house to make them live car-free for a month was too small-scale. A neighborhood was deemed to be the right size.

But how to identify a neighborhood, whose residents would voluntarily live without their cars? Who would be open to an experiment?

Suwon City conducted a process of competitive identification of the most appropriate project neighborhood. Together, the city and ICLEI defined selection criteria and three neighborhoods were assessed. In the end, Haenggung-dong was chosen.

Lebendiges Suwon

Suwon – 1,2 Millionen Einwohner, Hauptstadt von Südkoreas größter Provinz Gyeonggi, die die Landeshauptstadt Seoul umschließt.

Suwon ist ein Ausbildungszentrum mit elf Universitäten, ein industrieller Knoten mit dem Hauptsitz von Samsung Electronics und dessen Forschungs- und Entwicklungszentrum sowie eine beliebte Touristendestination aufgrund der Festung Hwaseong, der einzigen erhaltenen vollständig mit einem Festungswall umschlossenen Stadt Südkoreas, die als UNESCO-Weltkulturerbe geführt wird.

Ein besuchender Stadtplaner würde Suwon außerhalb des historischen Kerns als typische koreanische Stadt mit modernen, dicht mit Hochhäusern bebauten Wohnquartieren wahrnehmen. Ein Verkehrsplaner mag Suwon als Stadt der Autos und Busse sehen.

Suwons politische Führung ist stets darauf bedacht gewesen, Umweltinitiativen zu ergreifen und die Stadt zu einem international beachteten Akteur zu machen. Suwon schloss sich 2005 ICLEI, dem weltgrößten Städtenetzwerk für nachhaltige Entwicklung, an, war Gastgeber internationaler Umweltkonferenzen und ihr derzeitiger Bürgermeister Tae-young Yeom sitzt in ICLEIs Aufsichtsgremien. Suwon zielt auf nichts Bescheideneres, als Koreas Ökohauptstadt zu werden.

Auswahl eines Stadtquartiers

Wie lässt sich eine ökomobile Stadt schaffen? Alle Autos für einen gesamten Monat aus einer ganzen Stadt zu verbannen, erschien unrealistisch. Mit den Bewohnern eines einzelnen Hauses zu arbeiten, um sie autofrei leben zu lassen, war zu kleinmaßstäblich. Ein Stadtquartier wurde als richtige Größenordnung erachtet.

Aber wie ein Quartier mit Bewohnern finden, die freiwillig ohne Auto leben würden? Wer wäre offen gegenüber einem solchen Experiment?

Die Stadt Suwon organisierte einen Wettbewerb unter den Quartieren. Die Stadt und ICLEI definierten Entscheidungskriterien, und drei Quartiere wurden bewertet. Schließlich wurde Haenggung-dong ausgewählt.

Haenggung-dong Rediscovered

Haenggung-dong is a place of history. When, King Jeongjo attempted to make Suwon the national capital in 1796, Hwaseong Fortress, a fortified wall running around the entire city, was built—today a designated UNESCO World Heritage Site. The fortress area was the very center of the city. It still prospered even during the nineteen-sixties and -seventies. Triggered by the Korean economic boom, from the mid-nineteen-seventies, Korea's residents started moving into newly developed areas with modern housing. This also happened in Suwon, and the old town encircled by the Fortress began to decline.

Haenggung-dong is a neighborhood within the Paldal-gu District. It is administratively served by a subdistrict office, the Haenggung-dong Residents Autonomy Center. Haenggung-dong comprises several communities, out of which Sinpung-dong and Jangan-dong were chosen as the festival neighborhoods, because they present the center of Haenggung-dong while exhibiting the worst decline. The EcoMobility Festival area was encircled by Haenggung Palace and Haenggung Plaza in the South, the Fortress wall in the West and North, and the busy Jeongjo Street in the east.

Wiederentdecktes Haenggung-dong

Haenggung-dong ist ein geschichtsträchtiger Ort. Als im Jahre 1796 König Jeongjo den Versuch unternahm, Suwon zur nationalen Hauptstadt zu machen, wurde die Festung Hwaseong, eine befestigte, rund um die Stadt verlaufende Mauer, gebaut – heute als UNESCO-Weltkulturerbe ausgewiesen. Der Festungsbereich war bis hinein in die 1960er und 70er Jahre das prosperierende Zentrum der Stadt. Mit dem koreanischen Wirtschaftsaufschwung Mitte der 1970er Jahre wurden vielerorts neue, moderne Wohnsiedlungen errichtet – auch in Suwon, sodass die von der Mauer umschlossene Altstadt zu verfallen begann.

Haenggung-dong ist ein Quartier im Stadtteil Paldal-gu. Es wird verwaltungsmäßig durch ein Quartiersbüro bedient, das den Namen „Autonomiezentrum für die Bewohner Haenggung-dongs" trägt. Haenggung-dong besteht aus mehreren Ortsteilen, von denen Sinpung-dong und Jangan-dong als Festivalgebiet ausgewählt wurden, weil sie den zentralen Bereich Haenggungdongs darstellen und den schlimmsten Verfall aufwiesen. Das Gebiet des EcoMobility-Festivals war umrahmt vom Haenggung-Palast und dem Haenggung-Platz im Süden, der Festungsmauer im Osten und Norden und der geschäftigen Jeongjo-Straße im Osten.

◁
The planners experienced the streets of Haenggung-dong with mixed feelings.
Streets are used by buses and vendors—but speedy and noisy buses are bad for the vendors and spoil the shopping experience.
Die Planer erlebten die Straßen von Haenggung-dong mit gemischten Gefühlen.
Straßen werden von Bussen und Verkäufern genutzt – aber schnelle und lärmende Busse sind schlecht für die Verkäufer und verderben das Einkaufserlebnis.

◁
The streets are also there for cyclists and for children to play. There was space dedicated for parked cars, but none specifically for bicycles or children.
Straßen sind ebenso für Radfahrer da und für Kinder zum Spielen. Es gab Parkplätze, aber keine Flächen für Fahrräder oder Kinder.

◁
Some streets needed to be addressed more urgently than others, beyond speed bumps and traffic cones. Shop owners had to understand that sidewalks are for pedestrians and not for the storage of garbage and goods, and that the façade of a shop should be as appealing as the friendly face of its owner.
Einige Straßen verdienten offensichtlich Aufmerksamkeit über Fahrbahnschwellen und Verkehrshütchen hinaus – Ladenbesitzer sollten verstehen, dass Gehwege für Fußgänger da und keine Lagerflächen für Müll und Material sind, und dass die Fassade eines Geschäfts nicht weniger wirkt als das freundliche Gesicht des Besitzers.

❝ We visited and evaluated three areas that had expressed their interest. The city finally decided in favor of Haenggung-dong.
When we visited Haenggung-dong, we saw a fairly rundown area that was part of the old town. It was a historic jewel, admittedly neglected, however it had potential. It was obvious that this neighborhood could be energized, and in the end what we expected happened. ❞
Santhosh Kodukula,
EcoMobility Team Leader at ICLEI

❞ Wir besuchten und bewerteten drei Gebiete, die ihr Interesse bekundet hatten. Die Stadt entschied sich schließlich für Haenggung-dong.
Als wir Haenggung-dong besuchten, sahen wir ein ziemlich heruntergekommenes Gebiet, das Teil der Altstadt war. Es war ein historisches Juwel, zwar vernachlässigt, aber dennoch mit Potenzial. Es war offensichtlich, dass diesem Gebiet neue Energie eingeflößt werden könnte und zum Schluss erfüllte sich, was wir erwartet hatten. ❝
Santhosh Kodukula,
Teamleiter für EcoMobility bei ICLEI

Haenggung-dong's Wheeling Economy

Before long, the planners became familiar with the "Yogurt Lady," the "Paper Lady," the "Recycling Man," and the "Toilet Paper Man," who not only play an important role in maintenance and waste disposal, but who also move in a traditional, simple, ecomobile fashion. They felt that these people deserved a more modern ecomobile solution.

Haenggung-dongs Wirtschaftsleben auf Rädern

Bald wurden die Planer vertraut mit der „Joghurtfrau", der „Papierdame", dem „Recyclingmann" und dem „Klopapiermann" ..., die alle nicht nur eine wichtige Rolle in der Versorgung und Müllentsorgung spielen, sondern sich in einer traditionellen, schlichten, ökomobilen Weise bewegen. Diese Leute hatten eine modernere Ökomobilitätslösung verdient.

△
Daily transport
Alltäglicher Transport

△
Collection of recyclables
Sammlung von Wiederverwertbarem

△
EcoMobility offers for kids at a Haenggung-dong retailer
Ökomobilitäts-Angebote für Kinder bei einem Händler in Haenggung-dong

▽
With great joy, the planners noticed that people wanted to enjoy life outdoors—the best basis for street cafés!
Mit großer Freude stellten die Planer fest, dass es die Leute danach verlangte, sich draußen ihres Lebens zu erfreuen – beste Voraussetzungen für Straßencafés!

▷
The planners observed what the smaller city residents need in order to grow up and be part of a capable, future society—room to move, opportunities to unfold, space to develop creativity.
Die Planer bemerkten, was die kleinen Stadtbewohner brauchen, um aufzuwachsen und eine fähige zukünftige Gesellschaft zu formen – Bewegungsraum, Gelegenheiten sich zu entfalten, Raum, um Kreativität zu entwickeln.

Organization of the Work
Organisation der Arbeit

The EcoMobility Festival project began in early 2012. Suwon City and ICLEI agreed to share responsibilities and tasks. Suwon would take charge of the local organization, while ICLEI would be responsible for conceptual advice, international outreach, and communication, as well as the EcoMobility Congress that would take place during the festival.

A planning workshop in January 2012 marked the start of the project implementation. The festival team defined nine work streams with fifty-two work packages:

1: Citizens and Partners Engagement
2: Ground Implementation
3: Products Management (Vehicles)
4: Festival Program
5: Marketing, Promotion, and Tourism
6: Press and Media
7: Documentation and Reporting
8: Financial Resource Mobilization
9: Project Management and Coordination

The Mayor established an organizing committee to garner participation and support from a variety of organizations, and to organize the festival preparations efficiently and effectively. An Executive Committee served as coordinating body and took principle decisions by consensus.

These committees involved the mayor, vice mayors and district mayor, Creative Director of the festival, national parliamentarians as well as representatives of the City Council, several municipal departments, the police, the Haenggung-dong Residents Group, civil society organizations, the Korean Chamber of Commerce and, of course, UN-HABITAT and ICLEI.

Das Projekt des EcoMobility World Festival begann Anfang 2012. Die Stadt Suwon und ICLEI vereinbarten, die Verantwortlichkeiten und Aufgaben unter sich aufzuteilen. Suwon würde für die örtliche Organisation und ICLEI würde für die konzeptionelle Beratung, die internationale Öffentlichkeitsarbeit sowie den EcoMobility-Kongress verantwortlich sein, der während des Festivals stattfinden sollte.

Ein Planungsworkshop im Januar 2012 markierte den Start der Projektarbeiten. Das Festivalteam definierte neun Arbeitsbereiche mit 52 Arbeitspaketen:

1: Beteiligung von Bürgern und Partnern
2: Maßnahmen im Straßenraum
3: Produktmanagement (Fahrzeuge)
4: Festivalprogramm
5: Marketing, Werbung und Tourismus
6: Presse und Medien
7: Dokumentation und Berichterstattung
8: Mobilisierung finanzieller Ressourcen
9: Projektmanagement und Koordinierung

Der Bürgermeister berief einen Organisationsausschuss, um eine Beteiligung und Unterstützung durch eine Vielfalt von Organisationen zu sichern und die Festivalvorbereitungen effizient und wirksam zu organisieren. Ein Lenkungsausschuss fungierte als Koordinierungsgremium und traf Entscheidungen per Konsens.

Diese Gremien involvierten Bürgermeister, Vizebürgermeister und Bezirksbürgermeister, Festival-Kreativdirektor, nationale Parlamentarier sowie Vertreter des Stadtrats, verschiedener städtischer Ämter, der Polizei, der Einwohnervereinigung von Haenggung-dong, von Verbänden der Zivilgesellschaft, der Handelskammer und natürlich von UN-HABITAT und ICLEI.

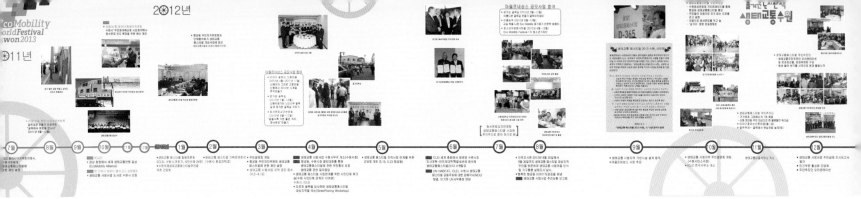

A Complex Process: Festival Timeline
Ein komplexer Prozess: Festival-Zeitschiene

1. Festival Idea and Conception

October 2011—ICLEI's first EcoMobility World Congress is held in Changwon, South Korea; the EcoMobility Alliance is launched / Suwon announces its intention to host EcoMobility World Festival 2013 / Haenggung-dong residents request Hwaseomun Street improvements at city budget roundtable

January 2012—First ICLEI-Suwon festival planning workshop

February 2012—Suwon begins the process of selecting the festival neighborhood together with residents' committees / a group of Haenggung-dong residents applies to host the festival

April 2012—Formation of the Festival Secretariat in Suwon / street planning workshop by Suwon City, ICLEI, and UN-Habitat

June 2012—Memorandum of Understanding signed between the three project partners (ICLEI, Suwon City, and UN-Habitat) at the ICLEI World Congress in Belo Horizonte, Brazil; first international media announcement of the festival issued

September 2012—Establishment of the Haenggung-dong Residents Group at the celebration of D-365 for the festival

2. Consultation—
Persuading over 4,300 Residents to Make the Switch

July 2012—Cooperative of Hwaseomun Street shop owners announce their support for the festival

August 2012—Residents informed about the festival and all households surveyed on awareness of the festival and mobility patterns and needs carried out / some faith is lost in the city administration due to the way the decision-making on the relocation of Sinpung Elementary School was handled / Village Renaissance Contest among residents groups takes place, producing neighborhood improvement ideas on the occasion of the festival

1. Festivalidee und -konzeption

Oktober 2011 – ICLEIs erster EcoMobility-Weltkongress wird in Changwon, Südkorea abgehalten; die EcoMobility-Allianz wird gegründet / Suwon kündigt seine Absicht an, das EcoMobility World Festival 2013 zu veranstalten / bei einem Runden Tisch der Stadt Suwon erbitten die Bewohner von Haenggung-dong Verbesserungen an der Hwaseomun-Straße

Januar 2012 – Erster Planungsworkshop von ICLEI und Suwon

Februar 2012 – Suwon startet gemeinsam mit Bewohnergremien das Auswahlverfahren für ein Stadtquartier für das Festival / eine Gruppe von Einwohnern von Haenggung-dong (HRG) bewirbt sich um die Veranstaltung des Festivals

April 2012 – Errichtung des Festivalsekretariats in Suwon / Straßenplanungsworkshop von Stadt Suwon, ICLEI und UN-Habitat

Juni 2012 – Absichtserklärung zwischen den drei Projektpartnern (ICLEI, Suwon, UN-Habitat) anlässlich des ICLEI-Weltkongresses in Belo Horizonte, Brasilien, unterzeichnet; erste internationale Medienankündigung des Festivals ausgesandt

September 2012 – Gründung der Einwohnervereinigung von Haenggung-dong bei der D-365-Feier für das Festival

2. Konsultation –
Über 4300 Bewohner werden überzeugt, sich umzustellen

Juli 2012 – Eine Kooperative der Ladenbesitzer an der Hwaseomun-Straße kündigt ihre Unterstützung des Festivals an

August 2012 – Bewohner werden über das Festival informiert und eine Befragung aller Haushalte über die Wahrnehmung des Festivals und der Mobilitätsmuster und -bedürfnisse wird durchgeführt / einiges Vertrauen in die Stadtverwaltung wird verspielt wegen der Art und Weise, wie über die Verlegung der Sinpung-Grundschule entschieden wurde / Dorfrenaissance-Wettbewerb unter Bewohnergruppen erbringt Ideen für die Quartiersverbesserung anlässlich des Festivals

October 2012—During the "Street Playground" event, residents walk in a car-free street for the first time / briefing session for residents
November 2012—Establishment of the neighborhood office
December 2012—Formation of the HRG Steering Committee and subcommittees / residents' meeting / Festival Organizing Committee moves to Haenggung-dong
January 2013—Joint ICLEI-Suwon work meeting
February 2013—Joint ICLEI-Suwon work meeting / opponents of the festival begin their Thursday assemblies

3. Urban Regeneration Works and Warming up for the Festival
March 2013—Urban regeneration works begin on Hwaseomun Street and Sinpung Street, with alley repaving and sewage system improvements / Haenggung-dong Festival Office explains details to residents through a series of neighborhood meetings
April 2013—Pocket park construction starts / first EcoMobility Forum / fourth ICLEI-UN-Habitat-Suwon workshop / citizens' bike school starts offering bicycle riding classes / car-free days take place in Hwaseomun Street, Jeongjo Street, and Haenggung Plaza
May 2013—Volunteers paint murals / Tong-tong managers (block representatives), together with HRG representatives, visit every household to promote festival
June 2013—Façade improvements commence / the urban renewal ("City Renaissance") project kicks off / a temporary parking lot is prepared / training for EcoMobility translation volunteers and neighborhood tour guide volunteers begins
July 2013—Another car-free day helps get residents in the mood / velotaxis start operating / a further ICLEI-Suwon work meeting takes place
August 2013—A number of "Liberation from Cars" events are held; the symbolic removal of about one hundred cars from the neighborhood is staged / overhead cabling in Hwaseomun & Sinpung Streets is transferred under-

Oktober 2012 – Während der „Straßenspielplatz"-Veranstaltung spazieren die Bewohner erstmals auf einer autofreien Straße / Informationssitzung für Bewohner
November 2012 – Errichtung des Quartiersbüros
Dezember 2012 – Errichtung des HRG-Lenkungsausschusses und der Unterausschüsse / Einwohnerversammlung / das Organisationskomitee für das Festival zieht nach Haenggung-dong um
Januar 2012 – Gemeinsame Arbeitssitzung ICLEI-Suwon
Februar 2012 – Gemeinsame Arbeitssitzung ICLEI-Suwon / die Gegner des Festivals beginnen ihre Donnerstagsversammlungen

3. Stadterneuerungsarbeiten und Warmlaufen für das Festival
März 2013 – Stadterneuerungsarbeiten beginnen in den Straßen Hwaseomun-ro und Sinpung-ro; dabei werden das Abwassersystem überholt und die Gassen neu gepflastert / das Festivalbüro in Haenggung-dong erläutert den Bewohnern Einzelheiten in einer Serie von Quartierstreffen
April 2013 – Der Bau von „Pocket Parks" beginnt / erstes EcoMobility-Forum / vierter ICLEI-UN-Habitat-Suwon-Workshop / Bürgerradfahrschule startet Angebot an Radfahrkursen / autofreie Tage finden in der Hwaseomun-Straße, der Jeongjo-Straße und auf dem Haenggung-dong Plaza statt
Mai 2013 – Freiwillige malen Wandmalereien / Tong-tong-Manager (Blockbeauftragte) und HRG-Vertreter besuchen jeden Haushalt, um für das Festival zu werben
Juni 2013 – Beginn der Fassadenverschönerung / das Stadterneuerungsprojekt („City Renaissance") startet / ein temporärer Parkplatz wird hergerichtet / Beginn der Ausbildung von Freiwilligen als Übersetzer und Quartierstourenführer
Juli 2013 – Ein weiterer autofreier Tag hilft Bewohnern, sich einzustimmen / Velotaxis nehmen den Betrieb auf / ein weiteres ICLEI-Suwon-Arbeitstreffen findet statt
August 2013 – Einige Veranstaltungen zur „Befreiung von Autos" werden abgehalten; die symbolische Entfernung von rund 100 Autos aus dem Quartier

ground / a neighborhood creation network is formed with the cooperation of Hwaseomun-Street shop owners, the association of shop owners in Hwaseomun and Sinpung Streets, the citizens' bike school, as well as alley magazine *Cider* / EcoMobility Forum on the festival legacy / Asia-Pacific EcoMobility Youth Forum gets underway

4. The Festival

September 2013—Celebrating the ecomobile neighborhood for the full month / opening ceremony on Haenggung-dong Plaza / Jeongjo-ro converted into "EcoMobility Street" for eight days / EcoMobility Parade / EcoMobility World Congress / EcoMobility vehicles exhibition / dozens of thematic and cultural events / blindfolded tour of the neighborhood every Saturday / physically impaired tour / Fiftieth Suwon Hwaseong Cultural Festival and Parade

October 2013—EcoMobility Idea Contest awards ceremony / Suwon NGO Forum on Post-Festival strategy / Post-Festival workshop with "Shinhwa Majunet," an active residents' group / formation of a network of café and cultural handicraft shop owners November 2013—Mayor invites Haenggung-dong residents to a round table with the topic, "A Discussion about the Sustainable Implementation of EcoMobility"

March 2014—Suwon City convenes second round table for Suwon citizens and stakeholders on city-wide transport policy; participants consider expansion of EcoMobility policy as a priority

wird in Szene gesetzt / die Freiluftleitungen in den Straßen Hwaseomun-ro und Sinpung-ro werden im Boden verlegt / ein Quartiersgestaltungs-Netzwerk wird gebildet durch Zusammenarbeit der Genossenschaft der Ladenbesitzer der Hwaseomun-Straße, der Ladenbesitzervereinigung von Hwaseomun-ro und Sinpung-ro, der Bürgerradfahrschule sowie dem Gassenmagazin *Cider* / EcoMobility-Forum über das Vermächtnis des Festivals / Asiatisch-Pazifisches EcoMobility-Jugendforum auf den Weg gebracht

4. Das Festival

September 2013 – Das ökomobile Stadtquartier wird einen vollen Monat lang begangen / Eröffnungszeremonie auf dem Haenggung-dong Plaza / die Jeongjo-Straße wird für acht Tage in die „EcoMobility-Straße" verwandelt / EcoMobility-Umzug / EcoMobility-Weltkongress / EcoMobility-Fahrzeugausstellung / Dutzende thematischer und kultureller Veranstaltungen / jeden Samstag Quartierstour mit verbundenen Augen / Rollstuhltour / 50. Suwoner Hwaseong-Kulturfest und Parade

Oktober 2013 – Preisverleihung beim EcoMobility-Ideenwettbewerb / Suwoner Verbändeforum zur Festival-Folgestrategie / Post-Festival-Workshop mit „Shinwa Majunet", einer aktiven Einwohnergruppe / Bildung eines Netzwerks der Inhaber von Cafés und Kulturhandwerksläden

November 2013 – Der Bürgermeister lädt Bewohner von Haenggung-dong zu einem Runden Tisch zum Thema „Gespräch über die nachhaltige Einführung von Ökomobilität" ein

März 2014 – Die Stadt Suwon lädt Bürger und Interessensvertreter zum zweiten Runden Tisch über die gesamtstädtische Verkehrspolitik ein; die Teilnehmer betrachten die Ausweitung des Ökomobilitäts-Programms als Priorität

4,343 residents involved

1 million visits attracted

7 million invested

area of **63** football fields

40 international businesses involved

1,500 vehicles removed

visitors from **50** countries

◁
The Festival:
Results of Twenty Months of
Planning and Preparation
Das Festival:
Ergebnis von 20 Monaten an
Planung und Vorbereitung

Yeonhee Park

A champion of the festival. Director of ICLEI's Korea Office, which is based in Suwon. Led the festival project until the city formed a team and appointed a city official to lead the project.

The ICLEI Korea Office became the temporary headquarters of the festival's Creative Director, an important place of exchange, consultation, and decision-making. Was it a lucky coincidence that ICLEI had moved its Korea Office to Suwon? No. It was Mayor Tae-young Yeom's vision of a globally connected city with superior quality of life for its residents that made him undertake both: attracting ICLEI's office and hosting the festival. The Korea Office also successfully co-organized the EcoMobility 2013 Congress.

Yeonhee Park

Champion des Festivals. Direktorin von ICLEI's Korea-Büro in Suwon. Leitete das Festivalvorhaben, bis die Stadt ein Team aufgestellt und einen Mitarbeiter mit der Projektleitung betraut hatte.

Das ICLEI-Korea-Büro wurde zum zeitweisen Hauptquartier des Festival-Kreativdirektors, ein wichtiger Ort des Austausches, der Konsultationen und Entscheidungen. War es ein glücklicher Zufall, dass ICLEI sein Korea-Büro nach Suwon verlegt hatte? Nein. Es war Bürgermeister Tae-young Yeoms Vision einer global vernetzten Stadt und erstklassiger Lebensqualität für die Bewohner, die ihn beides unternehmen ließ: das ICLEI-Büro anzusiedeln und das Festival zu organisieren. Das Korea-Büro organisierte auch erfolgreich den Kongress „EcoMobility 2013" mit.

❝ Yeonhee has become my good colleague, friend, advisor, supporter and—in the best sense—interpreter. She not only interpreted the Korean language for me, but also Korean culture, habits, personalities, and organizations. She has also arranged important appointments, accompanied me to meetings and events, and often not only translated my words, but also explained and interpreted my ideas, intention, goals, objectives, and concerns.

Without Yeonhee, I could not have explained the idea of the EcoMobility World Festival in a compelling way to Mayor Yeom, when we spoke first in Bonn. Without her, I would not have been introduced to so many actors in the Haenggung-dong neighborhood: writers, poets, artists, musicians, community activists, shop owners, hairdressers, recycling business owners, and logistic company directors. Without working together we could not have turned critical businessmen into friends and allies. ❞

Konrad Otto-Zimmermann

❞ Yeonhee ist mir eine gute Kollegin, Freundin, Beraterin, Unterstützerin und – im besten Sinne – Übersetzerin geworden. Sie hat mir nicht nur die koreanische Sprache, sondern koreanische Kultur, Gewohnheiten, Menschen und Organisationen interpretiert. Sie hat auch wichtige Treffen arrangiert, mich zu Sitzungen und Veranstaltungen begleitet und oft nicht nur meine Worte übersetzt, sondern meine Ideen, Intentionen, Ziele und Anliegen erklärt.

Ohne Yeonhee hätte ich die Idee des EcoMobility World Festivals niemals in überzeugender Weise Bürgermeister Yeom nahebringen können, als wir das erste Mal in Bonn darüber sprachen. Ohne sie wäre ich nicht so vielen Akteuren im Stadtquartier Haenggung-dong vorgestellt worden: Autoren, Dichtern, Künstlern, Musikern, Stadtteilaktivisten, Ladenbesitzern, Friseusen, Recyling-Geschäftsmännern, Direktoren von Transportunternehmen … Ohne die Zusammenarbeit mit ihr hätten wir nicht kritische Geschäftsleute zu Freunden des Festivals machen können. ❝

Konrad Otto-Zimmermann

Director
Direktor

Heung-soo Park

Serving as Suwon City's Director of Transportation, Mr. Heung-soo Park was appointed to lead the EcoMobility Festival project in its last, critical phase. While the festival was going on, Mr. Park lent his ear to the residents and business community. At the same time, he sought advice from international experts in an effort to prepare the City's legacy from the festival. He convened municipal departments and transport planners for two sessions and explained Suwon's strategy for advancing EcoMobility in the years to come.

Heung-soo Park

Der Direktor der Verkehrsabteilung der Stadt Suwon, Heung-soo Park, wurde in der letzten, kritischen Phase zum Leiter des EcoMobility-Festivalprojekts berufen.
Während das Festival lief, schenkte Herr Park sein Ohr den Bewohnern und der Geschäftswelt. Gleichzeitig suchte er Rat von internationalen Experten in dem Bestreben, die Hinterlassenschaft des Festivals für die Stadt zu planen. Er lud städtische Abteilungen und Verkehrsplaner zu zwei Sitzungen ein und erklärte Suwons Pläne dafür, Ökomobilität in den nächsten Jahren voranzubringen.

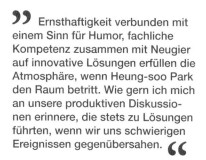

" Seriousness combined with a sense of humor, technical competence together with curiosity for innovative solutions fills the atmosphere when Heung-soo Park enters the room. How gladly I remember our productive discussions, which always led to solutions when we were facing critical events. **"**

Yeonhee Park

" Ernsthaftigkeit verbunden mit einem Sinn für Humor, fachliche Kompetenz zusammen mit Neugier auf innovative Lösungen erfüllen die Atmosphäre, wenn Heung-soo Park den Raum betritt. Wie gern ich mich an unsere produktiven Diskussionen erinnere, die stets zu Lösungen führten, wenn wir uns schwierigen Ereignissen gegenübersahen. **"**

Yeonhee Park

At the beginning of 2012, a small team of city officials worked in a dedicated festival office in City Hall. The team grew and was restructured several times, reflecting the increasing complexity of the endeavor and differentiation of tasks. In the end, twenty-eight staff members were part of the local festival team: nineteen city officials, four community, and five civil society representatives. ICLEI's international and Korean teams brought another ten people to the festival workforce.

The city's festival team—under the direction of Suwon City's Director of Transportation and Safety, Mr. Heung-soo Park, and Festival Director Byeong-Ik Kim—comprised the following subteams:
- Residents' Support
- Infrastructure and Transportation
- Festival Events and Cultural Programs
- Administrative Support and Public Relations

Anfang 2012 arbeitete ein kleines Team von städtischen Bediensteten in einem eigenen Festivalbüro im Rathaus. Das Team wuchs und wurde mit der wachsenden Komplexität des Unterfangens und der Ausdifferenzierung der Aufgaben mehrere Male umstrukturiert.

Zum Schluss waren 28 Mitarbeiter Teil des Festivalteams: 19 städtische Bedienstete, vier Einwohner- und fünf Vertreter der Zivilgesellschaft. ICLEIs internationales und koreanisches Team brachte weitere zehn Leute in die Festival-Mitarbeiterschaft ein.

Das städtische Festivalteam unter Leitung des Direktors für Verkehr und Sicherheit, Herrn Heung-soo Park, und des Festivaldirektors, Herrn Byeong-Ik Kim, umfasste folgende Teilteams:
- Unterstützung der Bewohner
- Infrastruktur und Verkehr
- Festivalveranstaltungen und Kulturprogramme
- Verwaltungsdienste und Öffentlichkeitsarbeit

▽
Mayor Yeom convened officials concerned with the festival for briefing meetings several times. The last session prior to the start of the festival with neighborhood representatives had the character of a roll-call review of the performance related to each task. We counted not less than 135 participants in the room.
Thirty-four divisions of the city administration and four city-related organizations—such as the Suwon Center for International Cooperation, Suwon Volunteers Center, Suwon Cultural Foundation and Suwon Local Agenda 21—contributed to the festival project.
Bürgermeister Yeom rief die mit dem Festival befassten Mitarbeiter mehrmals zu Briefing-Sitzungen zusammen. Die letzte Sitzung in der Woche vor Festivalbeginn mit Quartiersvertretern hatte den Charakter eines Appells, bei dem der Vollzugsstand für alle Aufgaben im einzelnen berichtet wurde. Wir zählten nicht weniger als 135 Beteiligte im Raum.
34 Abteilungen der Stadtverwaltung und vier stadtnahe Organisationen wie das Suwoner Zentrum für Internationale Zusammenarbeit, das Suwoner Freiwilligenzentrum, die Suwoner Kulturstiftung und Lokale Agenda 21 Suwon trugen zum Festivalprojekt bei.

▽
The teams from ICLEI and The Urban Idea in front of the ICLEI Korea Office in Suwon—the lovely office is the envy of ICLEI staff worldwide.
Die Teams von ICLEI und The Urban Idea vor dem ICLEI-Korea-Büro in Suwon – das hübscheste Büro, um das ICLEI-Mitarbeiter weltweit ihre koreanischen Kollegen beneiden.

△△
The Infrastructure and Transportation Team on-site visit in Haenggung-dong. The team's tasks included: reconstruction of Hwaseomun and Sinpung streets, repaving of alleys, removal of electric poles, arranging temporary parking lots for the cars of the residents, and their provision of EcoMobility vehicles.

Das Infrastruktur- und Verkehrsteam bei einem Ortstermin in Haenggung-dong. Seine Aufgaben: Umbau von Hwaseomun- und Sinpung-Straße, Neupflasterung der Gassen, Abbau der Strommasten, Herrichtung temporärer Parkplatzflächen für die Autos der Bewohner sowie deren Versorgung mit EcoMobility-Fahrzeugen

△
Always creative: Events and Cultural Programs Team. The team organized the opening and closing ceremonies, exhibitions, cultural performances, and participatory learning programs with residents.

Veranstaltungs- und Kulturprogrammteam. Es organisierte die Eröffnungs- und Schlusszeremonien, Ausstellungen, kulturelle Darbietungen und partizipative kulturelle Lernveranstaltungen mit Bewohnern.

△△
Administrative Support and Public Relations Team. The team worked with 240 City officials to reach out to all households with the festival newsletter *Green Messenger*; developed brochures, guidemap, and other materials; managed to get all cars removed from the neighborhood; responded to complaints raised by residents.

Verwaltungs- und Öffentlichkeitsarbeitsteam. Arbeitete mit 240 städtischen Bediensteten, um alle Haushalte mit dem Festivalblatt *Grüner Botschafter* zu erreichen. Entwickelte Broschüren, einen Übersichtsplan und andere Materialien. Schaffte es, alle Autos aus dem Quartier entfernt zu bekommen. Bearbeitete Beschwerden von Bewohnern.

△
The Residents' Support Team talking to a home-owner. This team organized and supported all festival-related activities of the Haenggung-dong Residents' Group. They also organized car-free days and the "Independence from Cars" event.

Das Einwohnerbetreuungsteam im Gespräch mit einem Hausbesitzer. Dieses Team organisierte und unterstützte alle festivalbezogenen Aktivitäten der Einwohnervereinigung von Haenggung-dong. Es organisierte auch autofreie Tage sowie die Veranstaltung zur „Unabhängigkeit von Autos".

Festival Headquarters

The festival office in central Haenggung-dong housed the workplaces of the City's local festival team, and hosted meetings with residents and business people, as well as project workshops. During the festival period, ICLEI's international festival team also moved into the building. The city had rented the space in order to make the festival organizers approachable by the public.

Festival-Hauptquartier

Das Festivalbüro im Zentrum Haenggung-dongs beherbergte die Arbeitsplätze des örtlichen Festivalteams der Stadt Suwon und diente als Ort für Treffen mit den Bewohnern und Geschäftsleuten sowie Projektworkshops. Während der Festivalperiode zog das internationale Festivalteam von ICLEI ebenfalls in das Haus ein. Die Stadt hatte die Räumlichkeiten angemietet, damit die Organisatoren des Festivals für die Öffentlichkeit ansprechbar waren.

◁
Vision of a redesigned street on a banner in front of the neighborhood office
Vision einer neu gestalteten Straße auf einem Banner vor dem Nachbarschaftsbüro

Relays: Paldal-gu and Haenggung-dong

The Paldal-gu District Office managed the reconstruction and improvement works for the neighborhood's streets and alleys, except for two main streets, which the Suwon city administration took care of. The office was in charge of safety and security, waste management, and residents' participation. District Mayor Geonmo Yoon (in the black suit) lent indispensable support to the festival organization.

The Haenggung-dong Village Office—positioned between the Suwon city administration and the residents—played a key role in the preparation and implementation of the EcoMobility World Festival. For the residents, office head Beomseon Lee (in the green jacket) and office secretary Ms. Jeongwan Lim were the first point of contact in all matters. The office provided logistical support to organizers and participants of the various events and served as relay concerning the participation of local leaders in events.

Relais: Paldal-gu und Haenggung-dong

Das Bezirksbüro von Paldal-gu leitete die Umbau- und Verschönerungsarbeiten für alle Straßen und Gassen des Quartiers außer den beiden Hauptstraßen, um die sich die Suwoner Stadtverwaltung kümmerte. Das Büro war zuständig für Sicherheit und Gefahrenabwehr, Abfallbeseitigung und Bürgerbeteiligung. Bezirksbürgermeister Geonmo Yoon (im schwarzen Anzug) gab dem Festival die unverzichtbare Unterstützung.

Das Dorfbüro von Haenggung-dong – zwischen der Stadtverwaltung von Suwon und den Bürgern verortet – spielte eine Schlüsselrolle bei der Vorbereitung und Umsetzung des EcoMobility World Festivals. Büroleiter Beomseon Lee (in grüner Jacke) und Bürosekretärin Jeongwan Lim waren für die Bewohner die erste Anlaufstelle in allen Angelegenheiten. Das Büro unterstützte die Veranstalter und Teilnehmer der verschiedenen Events logistisch und diente als Schnittstelle hinsichtlich der Beteiligung kommunaler Führungspersonen an Veranstaltungen.

A Festival by Citizens

Can you imagine a place where the *city administration* could produce a neighborhood whose residents would abandon their cars and live ecomobile for one month? It's indeed unthinkable. A project of this kind can only be implemented with and by the citizens. Suwon City therefore informed and involved the residents from the beginning.

- Local newspaper and TV reports
- Residents' assemblies
- Information büro flyers and neighborhood newsletters
- Resident surveys for all households
- Visits by residents' group to all households
- Establishment of a festival neighborhood office; the city paid for the rent and furniture, and residents operated the space as their office, meeting place, and information center
- The Suwon Festival Team and Organizing Committee operated from an office in the neighborhood and were thus approachable at any time

The residents and business people even organized themselves to help prepare for the festival:

- Formation of the Haenggung-dong Residents' Group, steering committee, and subcommittees
- Formation of several shop owners' associations
- Establishment of a "neighborhood creation network"

The scope of citizens and business engagement in the EcoMobility World Festival project by Suwon City was unprecedented in the country.

Ein Festival von Bürgern

Kann man sich einen Ort vorstellen, in dem die Stadtverwaltung ein Quartier schaffen könnte, dessen Bewohner für einen Monat ihr Auto aufgäben und ökomobil lebten? Das ist in der Tat undenkbar. Ein Projekt dieser Art kann nur mit den Bürgern und durch die Bürger durchgeführt werden. Die Stadt Suwon hat deshalb die Bewohner von Anfang an informiert und einbezogen.

- Berichte in örtlichen Zeitungen und im Fernsehen
- Einwohnerversammlungen
- Informationsblätter und Quartierszeitungen
- Bewohnerbefragungen bei allen Haushalten
- Besuche der Einwohnervereinigung bei allen Haushalten
- Einrichtung eines Festival-Quartiersbüros; die Stadt übernahm die Miete und Einrichtung, die Bewohner betrieben es als Büro, Versammlungsort und Informationszentrum.
- Das Suwoner Festivalteam und der Organisationsausschuss arbeiten von einem Büro im Quartier aus und sind dadurch jederzeit ansprechbar.

Bewohner und Geschäftsleute organisierten sich sogar selbst, um das Festival mit vorzubereiten:

- Bildung der Einwohnervereinigung von Haenggung-dong mit Lenkungsausschuss und Unterausschüssen
- Bildung mehrerer Vereinigungen von Geschäftsleuten
- Errichtung eines Netzwerks zur Gestaltung des Quartiers

Das Ausmaß an Bürger- und Wirtschaftsbeteiligung am EcoMobility World Festival durch die Stadt Suwon war beispiellos im Lande.

△
The neighborhood office at a crossing in central Haenggung-dong
Das Quartiersbüro an einer Kreuzung in der Mitte Haenggung-dongs

Paving the Road

❝ Even though the language and cultural 'barrier' presented an extra challenge for all parties involved, by focusing on our common goal we were successful. An important lesson that we learned: the active involvement and support of citizens during the entire project duration is crucial. Without their participation, there would have been no festival. ❞

Sophie Isabel Verstraelen, Project Administrator, EcoMobility World Festival

Den Weg bereiten

❞ Obwohl die sprachliche und kulturelle ‚Barriere' eine Herausforderung für alle Beteiligten war, waren wir erfolgreich durch unser gemeinsames Ziel. Eine wichtige Lektion, die wir lernten: Die aktive Beteiligung und Unterstützung durch die Bürger über die gesamte Projektdauer hinweg ist entscheidend. Ohne deren Mitwirkung hätte es kein Festival gegeben. ❝

Sophie Isabel Verstraelen, Projektadministratorin, EcoMobility World Festival

Ambassadors

Suwon City appointed three festival ambassadors, whose mandate was to spread the word about the Festival. Gil Peñalosa from 8-80 Cities inspired the Mayor, city councilors, officials, the festival team, and the public with a genuine fireworks display of interesting examples of progressive urban projects from cities on all continents, and he told the story of the festival to thousands of people in dozens of events worldwide. "Streets are for people, not for cars" was his key message. Famous Korean film actress Bo-young Park and radio moderator and TV actor Chul Park drew attention to the festival across the country.

Botschafter

Die Stadt Suwon ernannte drei Festivalbotschafter, deren Aufgabe es war, die Kunde vom Festival zu verbreiten. Gil Peñalosa von 8-80 Cities inspirierte den Bürgermeister, Stadträte, Beamte, das Festivalteam und die Öffentlichkeit mit einem wahren Feuerwerk interessanter Beispiele fortschrittlicher urbaner Projekte von Städten aus aller Welt, und er berichtete Tausenden von Menschen bei Dutzenden von Veranstaltungen in aller Welt vom Festival. „Straßen sind für die Menschen da, nicht für Autos" war seine Kernbotschaft. Die berühmte koreanische Filmschauspielerin Bo-young Park und Radiomoderator und Fernsehschauspieler Chul Park zogen landesweit Aufmerksamkeit auf das Festival.

Advisors

André Dzikus of UN-HABITAT (center) and the international advisors appointed by Suwon City—Gil Peñalosa (8-80 Cities, Toronto) and Florian Lennert (InnoZ, Berlin)—gave valuable technical advice on the design and implementation of the festival.

Berater

André Dzikus von UN-HABITAT (Bildmitte) und die von der Stadt berufenen internationalen Berater Gil Peñalosa (8-80 Cities, Toronto) und Florian Lennert (InnoZ, Berlin) gaben wertvolle fachliche Ratschläge zur Gestaltung und Umsetzung des Festivals.

△
The first visits by international experts and ICLEI's Festival team to Haenggung-dong were crucial because of two aspects: the planners were able to familiarize themselves with the neighborhood, the streets, buildings, the urban setting; and more importantly, they met and became friends with Suwon City officials, without whom the festival would never have succeeded.

Die ersten Besichtigungen Haenggung-dongs durch die internationalen Experten und ICLEIs Festivalteam waren aus zwei Gründen wichtig: Die Planer konnten sich mit dem Quartier, den Straßen, den Gebäuden und der städtebaulichen Struktur vertraut machen; und, wichtiger noch, sie lernten sich kennen und schlossen Freundschaften mit den städtischen Mitarbeitern, ohne die das Festival niemals ein Erfolg hätte werden können.

◁
The planning team walked and walked—and saw car after car, on lanes, on sidewalks, in narrow alleys, in front of shop doors… We were surprised to see so many oversized cars. Korean men have an average weight of 68.6, women of 56.5 kilograms. We saw drivers climb into SUVs and Vans of 2 to 5.5 tons. The tool they use for moving is thirty to forty-five times heavier than the driver—transport could not be more inefficient!

The planners tried to imagine how the streets would look and would be used if the cars disappeared.

Das Planungsteam ging und ging – und sah Autos über Autos, auf Fahrbahnen, auf Gehwegen, in engen Gassen, vor Ladentüren … Wir waren überrascht, so viele übergroße Autos zu sehen. Koreanische Männer wiegen durchschnittlich 68,6, Frauen 56,5 Kilogramm. Wir sahen Autofahrer in SUVs und Vans von 2 bis 2,5 Tonnen klettern. Das Gerät, das sie zur Fortbewegung nutzen, ist 30–45 mal schwerer als der Fahrer – Transport könnte nicht ineffizienter sein!

Die Planer versuchten sich vorzustellen, wie die Straßen aussehen und genutzt würden, wenn die Autos verschwunden wären.

◁
A lady in a mobility scooter came across our path. She was kind enough to share her reality with us: having to drive between the cars in the streets since either there are no sidewalks or they were too narrow because of poles, hydrants, and stalls, or blocked by parked cars.
Eine Dame in einem motorbetriebenen Scooter kam des Wegs. Sie war so nett, uns über ihre Realität zu erzählen: Sie muss zwischen den Autos auf der Straße fahren, weil es entweder keine Bürgersteige gibt oder diese durch Strommasten, Hydranten oder Verkaufsstände zu eng oder durch parkende Autos zugestellt sind.

▷
The festival team examined the load space of every truck, peered into every van, and spoke to shop owners in order to understand how local logistics were organized. How could urban freight transport be organized during the festival?
Das Festivalteam schaute auf die Ladefläche jedes Lastwagens und in jeden Lieferwagen und sprach mit Ladeninhabern, um zu verstehen, wie häufig sie mit welcher Ware beliefert werden. Wie könnte dies während des Festivals organisiert werden?

▽
Critical spots became soon apparent. How could a restaurant that specializes in catering to taxi drivers cope with a car-free month? A glimpse of the course of events reveals: initially, the owners of this restaurant opposed the festival project. Through dialogue with the city, an agreeable solution was found. In fact, the restaurant attracted so many visitors during the festival that the owners were more than satisfied in the end.
Kritische Punkte wurden bald offensichtlich. Wie könnte ein auf Taxifahrer spezialisiertes Restaurant mit einem autofreien Monat umgehen? Ein Blick auf den weiteren Verlauf der Dinge verrät: Die Besitzer bekämpften das Festivalprojekt zunächst, bis im Gespräch mit der Stadt eine annehmbare Lösung gefunden wurde. Und so adrett sah das Restaurant während des Festivals aus. Es zog so viele Besucher an, dass die Besitzer mit dem Ergebnis mehr als zufrieden waren.

What would Jeongjo-ro, the main four-lane arterial road bordering the neighborhood, look like during the Festival? Could it be converted into an EcoMobility street? A young artist drew a sketch of our vision.

Wie würde Jeongjo-ro, die vierspurige Hauptverkehrsstraße, die das Quartier begrenzt, während des Festivals aussehen? Könnte sie in eine EcoMobility-Straße verwandelt werden? Eine junge Künstlerin zeichnete einen Entwurf unserer Vision.

The city was determined to improve Hwaseomun-ro, the main street through Haenggung-dong. The proposed street design was presented to residents on a large tableau (photo, right) so that they could compare the present situation with the future option.

Die Stadt war entschlossen, Hwaseomun-ro, die Hauptstraße durch Haenggung-dong, aufzubessern. Die vorgeschlagene Straßengestaltung wurde den Bewohnern auf einem großen Wandbild (im Foto rechts) vorgestellt, sodass sie den heutigen Zustand mit der zukünftigen Alternative vergleichen konnten.

Declaration of Independence from Cars

Creativity without limits: a week before the festival started, Haenggung-dong residents began moving cars out of their neighborhood. The kick-off event was staged as a ceremony at which residents proclaimed a very special kind of independence declaration: The Declaration of Independence from Cars. Mayor Yeom encouraged the residents to follow through and complete the removal of cars by the Festival eve at midnight on August 31. A parade of ecomobile residents escorted the first cars that left the quarter.

Erklärung der Unabhängigkeit von Autos

Grenzenlose Kreativität: Eine Woche vor Festivalbeginn begannen Einwohner Haenggung-dongs, ihre Autos aus dem Gebiet zu entfernen. Die Auftaktveranstaltung wurde als eine Zeremonie inszeniert, bei der Bewohner eine sehr besondere Unabhängigkeitserklärung verkündeten: Die Erklärung der Unabhängigkeit von Autos. Bürgermeister Yeom ermutigte die Bewohner, das Wegparken der Autos bis zum Vorabend des Festivals, also bis Mitternacht des 31. August, zu bewerkstelligen. Ein Korso ökomobiler Bewohner eskortierte die ersten Autos, die das Quartier verließen.

Test Runs for the Big Event

With support from Suwon City, the Haenggung-dong Residents' Group and different groups of business people organized car-free Saturdays and Sundays and partied in the streets. Through these events, residents' support for the festival was drummed up, the neighborhood became familiar with car-free streets, and the organizers could see them as pilot runs for the big event.

Probeläufe für das große Ereignis

Die Einwohnervereinigung von Haenggung-dong und die verschiedenen Gruppen von Geschäftsleuten organisierten mit Unterstützung durch die Stadt Suwon autofreie Samstage und Sonntage und feierten auf der Straße. Durch diese Veranstaltungen wurde die Begeisterung der Bewohner für das Festival geweckt, das Quartier machte sich mit autofreien Straßen vertraut und die Veranstalter konnten sie als Probeläufe für das große Ereignis betrachten.

A Festival Is Not for Free

The Festival was certainly not cheap to organize. Looking at the budget, a distinction has to be made between two dimensions of the project. The character of the project as temporary mise en scène, "event," or better "multi-event" was one dimension. The long-term improvements, beautification, and reconstruction—which were triggered by the festival project—added another dimension. These were in fact implemented as part of a wider urban renewal effort and upgrade of the quarter, and can therefore not be attributed to the festival proper. The total budget was 11.25 billion Korean Won, corresponding to roughly 7.75 million euros or 10.45 million US dollars.

Two-thirds of the amount was invested in permanent infrastructure, such as road construction in two main streets, support of façade renovation, sewer renewal in alleys, and road/parking infrastructure. Such investment would have had to be made eventually in the area.

The rest was spent on the festival event proper. In particular, costs accrued for the civil secretariat (community office), international consulting and promotion, local and domestic communication and promotion, exhibition and congress pavilions, rental of shuttle vehicles, bicycles for residents, bicycle training for residents, EcoMobility vehicle sourcing internationally, car-free Saturdays and Sundays prior to the Festival, the EcoMobility Congress, further accompanying events and volunteers.

The vast part of the budget was borne by Suwon City.

Ein Festival gibt's nicht umsonst

Das Festival war sicherlich nicht billig zu veranstalten. Hinsichtlich des Budgets muss zwischen zwei Dimensionen des Projekts unterschieden werden. Der Charakter des Projekts als zeitweise *Inszenierung*, „Veranstaltung" oder besser „Multi-Event" war die eine Dimension. Die längerfristigen Verbesserungen, die Verschönerung und Sanierung, die durch das Festival ausgelöst wurden, fügten eine andere Dimension hinzu. Diese wurden als Teil einer weitergehenden Stadterneuerung und Aufwertung des Quartiers durchgeführt und können deshalb nicht dem eigentlichen Festival zugerechnet werden.

Das Gesamtbudget umfasste 11,25 Milliarden Koreanische Won, was etwa 7,75 Millionen Euro oder 10,45 Millionen US-Dollar entspricht.

Zwei Drittel dieses Betrags wurden in dauerhafte Infrastruktur wie Straßenbau in zwei Hauptstraßen, Fassadenrenovierungen, Kanalsanierungen in den Gassen sowie Straßen- und Parkierungsinfrastruktur investiert. Solche Ausgaben wären in diesem Gebiet ohnehin angestanden.

Der Rest wurde für das eigentliche Festival ausgegeben. Kosten entstanden insbesondere für das Bürgersekretariat (Nachbarschaftsbüro), internationale Beratung und Öffentlichkeitsarbeit, örtliche und landesweite Kommunikation und Öffentlichkeitsarbeit, Ausstellungs- und Kongresspavillons, Miete von Shuttle-Fahrzeugen, Fahrräder für die Bewohner, Fahrradunterricht für Bewohner, Beschaffung internationaler Fahrzeuge, Veranstaltung autofreier Samstage und Sonntage vor dem Festival, den EcoMobility-Kongress, weitere Begleitveranstaltungen und den Freiwilligendienst.

Der Großteil der Ausgaben wurde durch die Stadt Suwon getragen.

▷
Wishes from citizens for the festival displayed at the entrance of the Munhwa Cultural Super Market in Haenggung-dong
Wünsche der Bürger an das Festival, ausgehängt vor dem „Kultursupermarkt Munhwa" in Haenggung-dong

Thousands of Volunteers ...
Tausende Freiwilliger ...

△
Suwon City managed to recruit over a thousand volunteers from all over the city—and even countrywide—who provided vital services to the festival organizers, citizens, and guests.
Die Stadt Suwon schaffte es, über 1000 Freiwillige aus der gesamten Stadt und sogar landesweit zu gewinnen, die die Veranstalter, die Bürger und die Besucher mit wesentlichen Dienstleistungen unterstützten.

The Haenggung-dong community was far from unanimous in their perception of the festival and the benefits or damages it could bring. While a number of initially fairly vocal opponents later joined the promoters, a few continued to campaign against it—even on the opening day. Posters in showcases expressed the shop owners' protest against the closure of Jeongjo Street to private automobile traffic.

Die Einwohnerschaft von Haenggung-dong war bei weitem nicht einmütig in ihrer Einschätzung des Festivals und des Nutzens oder Schadens, die es bringen würde. Während eine Reihe von anfänglich lautstarken Gegnern später zu den Befürwortern überliefen, zogen andere weiterhin gegen das Projekt zu Felde – sogar noch am Eröffnungstag. Plakate in den Schaufenstern drücken den Protest der Geschäftsleute gegen die Schließung der Jeongjo-Straße für privaten Autoverkehr aus.

5,936 volunteers | **thereof** **3,648** guards at checkpoints (traffic regulation) | **1,446** information booths, velotaxi and shuttle drivers | **425** translators | **417** tourist and tour guides

From the selection of the neighborhood, to the planning and implementation of the EcoMobility World Festival—the political leadership of Suwon City considered the active participation and co-creation of the event by the Haenggung-dong residents a key success factor.

Von der Auswahl des Stadtquartiers über die Planung bis zur Durchführung des EcoMobility World Festivals – die politische Führung der Stadt Suwon erachtete die aktive Beteiligung und Mitschaffung der Veranstaltung durch die Bewohner von Haenggung-dong als wesentlichen Erfolgsfaktor.

Haenggung-dong Residents' Group (HRG)

As Suwon City searched for a neighborhood for the festival, the Paldal-gu district office initiated the formation of an official representative group of residents, who served as the applicant. The Haenggung-dong Residents' Group (HRG) was officially launched exactly one year before the start of the festival—and had at that time 180 members.

The HRG developed into the main representative organization and true host of the festival, because it was the residents who were intended to showcase an ecomobile way of life in their neighborhood. When the festival arrived, the HRG had 1,280 members—one-third of the population of Haenggung-dong!

The HRG appointed a Steering Committee and organized its work in eleven thematic subcommittees on matters such as EcoMobility, street beautification, community economy, community festival, communication, green lifestyle, alley academy, youth, and others.

HRG representatives were also a part of the Festival Organizing Committee, the main entity for decision-making. Whenever a conflict emerged, HRG members acted as mediators.

HRG members contributed actively as organizers, volunteer staff, performers or participants—whether as members of dancing groups, interviewers for the neighborhood survey, community guides, velotaxi drivers, or otherwise. That way, the HRG made residents take ownership of the event as civic hosts, allowing them to share the success and the fame of the world's first EcoMobility Festival.

After the festival, the HRG was dissolved. However, the active residents still form an informal band, which keeps the EcoMobility spirit in Haenggung-dong alive.

Einwohnervereinigung von Haenggung-dong (HRG)

Als die Stadt Suwon ein Stadtquartier für das Festival suchte, initiierte das Bezirksbüro von Paldal-gu die Bildung einer offiziellen Einwohnervertretung, die als Antragsteller fungierte. So entstand die Einwohnervertretung von Haenggung-dong (HRG), die exakt ein Jahr vor dem Festivalbeginn mit anfänglich 180 Mitgliedern gegründet wurde.

Die HRG entwickelte sich zur Hauptvertretungsorganisation und zur wahren Ausrichterin des Festivals, denn schließlich waren es ja die Bewohner, die eine ökomobile Lebensweise in ihrem Stadtquartier vorführen sollten. Zu Beginn des Festivals repräsentierte die HRG 1280 Mitglieder – ein Drittel aller Bewohner Haenggung-dongs!

Die HRG berief einen Leitungsausschuss und organisierte ihre Arbeit in elf thematischen Arbeitsgruppen um Fragen wie Ökomobilität, Straßenverschönerung, Quartiersökonomie, Nachbarschaftsfestival, Kommunikation, grüner Lebensstil, Gassen-Akademie, Jugend und andere.

HRG-Vertreter wirkten auch im Hauptentscheidungsgremium des Festivals mit. Wann immer ein Konflikt aufkam, fungierten die HRG-Mitglieder als Vermittler.

Mitglieder der HRG engagierten sich als Veranstalter, freiwillige Mitarbeiter, Darsteller oder Teilnehmer – ob als Mitglieder einer Tanzgruppe, als Interviewer bei der Bewohnerbefragung, als Quartierführer, als Velotaxifahrer oder anderweitig. So bewirkte die HRG, dass die Bewohner sich mit dem Ereignis identifizierten und am Erfolg und Ruhm des weltersten EcoMobility-Festivals teilhaben konnten.

Nach dem Festival wurde die HRG aufgelöst. Die aktiven Bewohner bilden jedoch noch immer eine informelle Gruppe, die den Geist der Ökomobilität in Haenggung-dong am Leben erhält.

Community Leader
Wortführer der Quartiersbewohner

Jong-ho Do

Chairman of Haenggung-dong Residents' Group. Senior resident of festival neighborhood. Successful businessman. Has been voluntarily serving the community for thirty years.
With the challenging festival project, Mr. Do became a pioneer of EcoMobility and a bike rider on rocky roads.

Jong-ho Do

Vorsitzender der Einwohnervereinigung von Haenggung-dong. Älterer Bewohner des Festivalquartiers. Erfolgreicher Geschäftsmann. Hat dem Gemeinwesen für 30 Jahre ehrenamtlich gedient.
Durch das schwierige Festivalprojekt wurde Herr Do zu einem Pionier der Ökomobilität und ein Radfahrer über steinige Wege.

Community Organizer
Nachbarschafts-Vernetzerin

Gyeong-ah Go

Appointed as a Neighborhood Director of the festival. Understanding the needs of the residents. Sympathizing with their sentiments.
She believes that the people in Haenggung-dong have paved a historic way towards a sustainable future. "The way they paved will certainly guide us to a better development."

Gyeong-ah Go

Ernannt zur Quartiersdirektorin für das Festival. Versteht die Bedürfnisse der Bewohner. Mitfühlend mit deren Stimmungen.
Sie glaubt, dass die Leute von Haenggung-dong einen historischen Pfad zu einer nachhaltigen Zukunft gelegt haben. „Der Weg, den sie bereitet haben, wird uns sicherlich zu einer besseren Entwicklung führen."

△
Ehwa Cho, owner of the traditional Korean restaurant Hwaseon-gok at Hwaseomun Street in central Haenggung-dong, and her mother were among the early promoters of the festival project. She spread the word about the event to garner support in the community, played an active role in a Shop Owners' Group, was active in the HRG, and thus it is no surprise that she could welcome many festival visitors as guests. "The Festival could have gone on forever," she says.

Ehwa Cho, Besitzerin des traditionellen koreanischen Restau-rants „Hwaseongok" an der Hwaseomun-Straße im Zentrum von Haenggung-dong, und ihre Mutter zählten zu den frühen Förderern des Festivalprojekts. Sie verbreitete die Kunde vom Festival, um Unterstützung innerhalb der Einwohnerschaft zu gewinnen, spielte eine tatkräftige Rolle in einem Verein der Geschäftsleute, war aktiv in der Haenggung-dong-Einwoh-nervereinigung, und so ist es keine Überraschung, dass sie viele Festivalbesucher als Gäste ihres Hauses begrüßen konnte. „Das Festival hätte für immer weitergehen können", sagt sie.

△
The business community of Haenggung-dong joined together in various groups according to type of business or location. They developed ideas for their participation in the festival, and the projects they proposed were reviewed by the city and, if selected, received modest financial support. Business groups managed the food court, organized street festivals in the months leading up to the big event, ran a booth where visitors could make candy by pedal power, and set up stalls in the streets.

Die Geschäftswelt von Haenggung-dong schloss sich zu ver-schiedenen Gruppen zusammen, je nach Wirtschaftszweig oder Lage. Sie entwickelten Ideen für ihre Beteiligung am Festival und die von ihnen vorgeschlagenen Projekte wurden von der Stadt geprüft und, falls ausgewählt, mit einem bescheidenen Betrag bezuschusst. Gruppen von Geschäftsleuten betrieben den Food Court, organisierten Straßenfeste in den Monaten vor dem großen Ereignis, betrieben einen Stand, bei dem Besucher mit Pedalkraft Zuckerwatte herstellen konnte, und stellten Verkaufs-stände in den Straßen auf.

△
Youngsoon Lee and her husband, owners of the drivers' restaurant Heemang (Hope) benefited from turning their initial opposition into cooperation. They made good business by using previous parking spots as outdoor seating areas and catering to festival visitors.
Youngsoon Lee und ihr Ehemann, Besitzer des Fahrerrestaurants „Heemag" (Hoffnung), gaben ihren Widerstand auf und kooperierten mit dem Festival – mit Gewinn: Sie machten ein gutes Geschäft mit der Nutzung der vorherigen Autoparkplätze als Freiluftsitzplätze und der Bewirtung von Festivalbesuchern.

△
Shop owner Youngmee Lee of Gogag Mart (Precious Customers' Mart) was a candid supporter of the festival project. She accepted that her merchandise was delivered to the temporary parking lot outside of the neighborhood, from where it was then couriered to her shop by the city's electric shuttle vehicle. The festival visitors constituted additional customers.
Ladenbesitzerin Youngmee Lee vom „Gogag Mart" (Geschätzte-Kunden-Markt) war eine aufrichtige Unterstützerin des Festivalprojekts. Sie akzeptierte, dass ihre Waren zunächst zum temporären Parkplatz geliefert und dann vom städtischen Elektro-Shuttlefahrzeug zu ihrem Geschäft transportiert wurden. Die Festivalbesucher stellten zusätzliche Kundschaft dar.

▷
High school students became "youth reporters": they interviewed residents, business people, and city officials, and wrote articles about all aspects regarding the Festival, which were published in a neighborhood newsletter that was distributed throughout the quarter.
Gymnasiasten wurden „Jugendredakteure": sie interviewten Bewohner, Geschäftsleute und städtische Bedienstete und schrieben Artikel über alle Aspekte rund um das Festival für eine Quartierszeitung, die im ganzen Stadtquartier verteilt wurde.

6 Makeover of a Quarter

Verschönerung eines Quartiers

Haenggung-dong was due to be rehabilitated and beautified. The Mayor of Suwon saw the EcoMobility World Festival as an ideal kickoff for the process of cautious urban renewal.

According to the idea and concept of the project, the festival should have been a temporary mise en scène: redecoration rather than reconstruction. Temporary provision of EcoMobility vehicles rather than their purchase on a permanent basis.

Yet, the Mayor determined that residents might feel that the city's intention to renew the quarter was not serious, if all changes made were temporary and reverted after one month. Therefore, the city invested in the permanent reconstruction of two main streets, the improvement of façades, the pavement and beautification of alleys, and the creation of "pocket parks" as lasting improvements—developed, designed, and implemented in cooperation with the residents, homeowners, and business people, as well as with the artists and craftsmen.

Die Erneuerung und Verschönerung von Haenggung-dong waren ohnehin fällig. Der Suwoner Bürgermeister sah das EcoMobility World Festival als einen idealen Auftakt für eine behutsame Stadterneuerung.

Entsprechend der Idee und dem Konzept des Projekts sollte das Festival eine zeitweise Inszenierung sein: Umdekorierung statt Umbau, zeitweise Bereitstellung von Fahrzeugen statt deren dauerhafte Beschaffung.

Dennoch fürchtete der Bürgermeister, dass die Bewohner an der Absicht der Stadt, das Quartier nachhaltig zu erneuern, zweifeln könnten, wenn alle Veränderungen nur temporär sein und nach einem Monat wieder zurückgenommen würden. Deshalb investierte die Stadt in den dauerhaften Umbau zweier Hauptstraßen, die Verschönerung der Fassaden, die Pflasterung und Verschönerung der Gassen und die Schaffung von „Pocket-Parks" als bleibende Verbesserungen – entwickelt, gestaltet und ausgeführt in Zusammenarbeit mit Bewohnern, Hausbesitzern und Geschäftsleuten sowie Künstlern und Handwerkern.

Haenggung-dong streets and alleys now looked neat and tidy. Alleys and stretches of streets had been paved, façades beautified, alley-side greenery planted, pocket parks created, murals painted, and space created—through the removal of the cars. Residents did not want to, and visitors could not, picture the previously car-packed streets and alleys any more.

Die Straßen und Gassen von Haenggung-dong sahen nun sauber und gepflegt aus. Gassen und Straßenabschnitte waren gepflastert, Straßenbegleitgrün gepflanzt, Miniparks angelegt, Wandbilder gemalt und Platz geschaffen – durch die Entfernung der Autos. Die Bewohner mochten, die Besucher konnten sich die zuvor mit Autos vollgepackten Straßen und Gassen nicht mehr vorstellen.

▷ Hwaseomun Street 2012 Die Hwaseomun-Straße im Jahr 2012

▷ CAD image of Hwaseomun Street design proposed by Suwon City, Spring 2013 CAD-Bild der von der Stadt Suwon vorgeschlagenen Gestaltung im Frühjahr 2013

▷ Hwaseomun Street after reconstruction following residents' preferences, September 2013 Die Hwaseomun-Straße nach dem Umbau entsprechend den Präferenzen der Bewohner, September 2013

Alleys redesigned with paving, alley-side planting

Façades improved with attractive shop signs

Mural art, street art

Pocket parks created

Plant containers as traffic dividers and barriers

Streets redesigned with paving, tree planting

Cables buried underground

**Beautification as a Means
to Enhance a Community's Self-esteem**

Suwon City's concept for the cautious urban renewal of Haenggung-dong included beautification projects. Burying electric cables underground, overhauling façades, creating "pocket parks" on small gap sites, planting colorful flowers, and choosing a meaningful design for infrastructure elements, such as bicycle racks—the range of measures undertaken to beautify the neighborhood satisfied residents and impressed visitors.

Verschönerung als Mittel zur Steigerung der Selbstachtung

Das Konzept der Stadt Suwon für die behutsame Stadterneuerung von Haenggung-dong schloss Verschönerungsvorhaben ein. Die Untergrundverlegung elektrischer Kabel, die Renovierung der Fassaden, die Anlage von Miniparks („Pocket Parks") in kleinen Baulücken, die Anpflanzung farbenprächtiger Blumen und das bedeutungsvolle Design von Infrastrukturelementen wie Fahrradständern – die Palette der Maßnahmen zur Verschönerung des Stadtquartiers hat die Bewohner zufriedengestellt und die Besucher beeindruckt.

Community Gardens

The laying out of three community gardens was part of the improvements to the Haenggung-dong quarter. Gap sites were transformed into gardens by the Agricultural Techno-logy Center—not only for urban farming, but also as environmental education site for citizens.

Gemeinschaftsgärten

Die Anlage von drei Gemeinschaftsgärten war Teil der Verbesserungen im Quartier Haenggung-dong. Baulücken wurden durch das Landwirtschaftliche Technologiezentrum in Gärten verwandelt – für *Urban Farming* und für ökologischen Anschauungsunterricht.

Political Urbanist
Politischer Urbanist

Jae-Joon Lee

Appointed as Second Vice Mayor of Suwon in 2011. Teaches Urban Planning and Regeneration as Professor at Hyupsung University. Advisor to local and central governments, Local Agenda 21 organizations, and NGOs.
As Co-chair of the Festival Executive Committee, Prof. Lee was responsible for the overall coordination across city bureaus, divisions, and people. He configured the festival as a combination of transport planning with urban planning and regeneration so that the festival process would become a new model of old town regeneration.

Jae-Joon Lee

Zum Vizebürgermeister von Suwon berufen im Jahr 2011. Lehrt Stadtplanung und -erneuerung als Professor an der Hyupsung-Universität. Berater von Kommunen und Regierung, Lokale-Agenda-21-Organisationen und Verbänden.
Als Ko-Vorsitzender des Festivalvorstands war Prof. Lee für die Gesamtkoordinierung der verschiedenen städtischen Ämter, Abteilungen und Akteure verantwortlich. Er konzipierte das Festival als eine Kombination von Verkehrsplanung mit Stadtplanung und -erneuerung, ein neues Modell von Altstadterneuerung.

❝ We were happy about every opportunity to debate on critical festival matters with Vice Mayor Lee—a conversation with him about our far- reaching ideas was always a reality check. While he developed enthusiasm for creative concepts, his political experience brought things back to the level of what is possible. We enjoyed working together. **❞**

Yeonhee Park and Konrad Otto-Zimmermann

❞ Wir waren froh über jede Gelegenheit, kritische Festivalangelegenheiten mit Prof. Lee zu erörtern – eine Unterhaltung mit ihm über unsere weitreichenden Ideen war immer ein Realitätscheck. Während er Enthusiasmus für kreative Konzepte entwickelte, führte seine politische Erfahrung die Dinge wieder auf den Boden des Machbaren zurück. Wir genossen es, zusammenzuarbeiten. **❝**

Yeonhee Park und Konrad Otto-Zimmermann

▽
2012

▽
September 2013

Culturalist
Kulturistin

The Culturalist and the Artists

The Haenggung-dong Artists Residency is a place where artists can stay and work in collaboration with residents. Most artists in the residency joined the Haenggung-dong Residents' Group to support the festival. The cultural team of the Festival Office enjoyed a partnership with the residency and worked closely with the artists on the planning and implementation of cultural activities. There were invaluable, voluntary contributions from the residency and Suwon-based artists, with strong support from the Festival Office.

Die Kulturistin und die Künstler

Die Künstlerresidenz von Haenggung-dong ist ein Ort, an dem Künstler wohnen und in Verbindung zu den Bewohnern arbeiten können. Die meisten Künstler in der Residenz schlossen sich der Einwohnervereinigung von Haenggung-dong an, um das Festival zu unterstützen. Das Kulturteam des Festivalbüros pflegte eine Partnerschaft mit der Residenz und arbeitete bei der Planung und Umsetzung kultureller Aktivitäten eng mit den Künstlern zusammen. Es gab unschätzbare freiwillige Beiträge von der Residenz wie auch von Künstlern aus Suwon mit starker Unterstützung durch das Festivalbüro.

> **“** Cultural Program Coordinator Youngran Noh of the Festival Team was the creative soul, the facilitator, and the manager of the rich cultural program during the month-long festival. Thus, with her, the festival became more colorful and enjoyable. **”**
>
> Yeonhee Park

> **”** Die Koordinatorin des Kulturprogramms, Youngran Noh vom Festivalteam, war die kreative Seele, Prozessbegleiterin und Managerin des reichhaltigen kulturellen Programms während des ganzmonatigen Festivals. Mit ihr wurde das Festival farbiger und amüsant. **“**
>
> Yeonhee Park

▽
The cultural group seizing the street
Die Kulturgruppe belegt die Straße

▽
Creative playground designed by the cultural group on a former parking lot
Kreativer Spielplatz, gestaltet von der Kulturgruppe auf einem früheren Parkplatz

“ Now it is more convenient to walk in the neighbor-hood. ”

” Jetzt ist es viel angenehmer, im Quartier zu Fuß zu gehen. “

“ The streets have been nicely refurbished. ”

” Die Straßen sind hübsch erneuert worden. “

“ The Festival is 'living education' for the children. ”

” Das Festival ist ‚lebende Erziehung' für die Kinder. “

 “ I like that people cooperate and meet in the streets. ”

” Ich mag es, dass die Leute zusammenarbeiten und sich auf der Straße treffen. “

7 EcoMobility Solutions
Ökomobilitäts-Lösungen

One Neighborhood—One Month—No Cars

This promise of the project was quite challenging. 1,500 cars had to be removed from the area in order to create free street space for EcoMobility and all sorts of cultural activities. Alternative ways of moving around and transporting merchandise had to be organized.

Ein Stadtquartier – ein Monat – autofrei

Dieses Versprechen des Projekts war recht herausfordernd. 1500 Autos mussten aus dem Gebiet entfernt werden, um freien Straßenraum für Ökomobilität und jegliche Art von kulturellen Aktivitäten zu schaffen. Alternative Arten der Fortbewegung und des Warentransports mussten organisiert werden.

Removal of Cars

The city administration prepared four abandoned lots as substitute parking lots for the cars from Haenggung-dong. Each vehicle owner was allotted a parking place free of charge.

The residents were informed about the parking arrangement several times; on the day before the festival began, they were once more reminded to remove their cars through a notice on the windshield.

If a car entered the area later against the arrangement, the car owner was asked to remove the car immediately from the area, with another notice on the windshield.

The Decisive Night

On the eve of the festival—August 31, 2013—youth groups celebrated the start of the festival with a candlelight ceremony, under a landmark tree below the wall of historic Hwaseong Fortress. City officials were roaming through the streets, noting the cars that still remained, ringing at doorbells or putting them on the list of phone calls for the next morning to urge owners to remove their cars.

Entfernung der Autos

Die Stadtverwaltung richtete vier Brachflächen als Ersatzparkflächen für die Autos aus Haenggung-dong her. Jedem Kraftfahrzeughalter wurde ein kostenfreier Parkpatz zugewiesen.

Die Bewohner wurden mehrfach über die Parkregelung informiert und am Tag vor Festivalbeginn noch einmal durch Zettel an den Windschutzscheiben gebeten, ihre Autos umzuparken.

Drang später ein Auto entgegen der Regelung in das Quartier ein, wurde der Halter durch eine weitere Notiz an der Windschutzscheibe dazu aufgefordert, das Auto umgehend aus dem Gebiet zu bringen.

Die entscheidende Nacht

Am Vorabend des Festivals – 31. August 2013 – feierten Jugendgruppen den Festivalbeginn mit einer Kerzenscheinzeremonie bei einem markanten Baum unterhalb der Stadtmauer der historischen Hwaseong-Festung. Städtische Bedienstete durchstreiften die Straßen und notierten, welche Autos noch immer verblieben waren; sie klingelten an den Haustüren oder setzten die Kfz-Halter auf die Liste für Telefonanrufe am nächsten Morgen, um sie zum Wegparken ihrer Autos zu drängen.

Keeping the Cars Out

The Haenggung-dong neighborhood would not have remained car-free if the city administration had not established checkpoints at all entries to the quarter. Not only signs and barriers kept cars out of the neighborhood—the city had recruited volunteers from the Best Drivers Association and from among the residents to serve at the checkpoints on a 24/7 basis. The thoroughfare was free for EcoMobility vehicles, and also for the official shuttle services between the car-free neighborhood and the temporary parking lots.

Thrilling stories were told about incidents where car drivers tried to force their way into the festival neighborhood, yelled at or accosted the watchmen at the checkpoints.

Die Autos draußen halten

Das Quartier Haenggung-dong wäre nicht lange autofrei geblieben, hätte die Stadtverwaltung nicht Kontrollpunkte an allen Einfahrten zum Bereich eingerichtet. Nicht nur Schilder und Schranken hielten Autos aus dem Quartier fern – die Stadt hatte Freiwillige vom Verein der Unfallfreien Fahrer und aus der Bewohnerschaft dazu rekrutiert, rund um die Uhr an den Kontrollpunkten Dienst zu tun. Die Durchfahrt war frei für Ökomobilitäts-Fahrzeuge und auch für die offiziellen Pendeldienste zwischen dem autofreien Quartier und den zeitweisen Parkplätzen.

Aufregende Geschichten wurden über Vorfälle erzählt, bei denen Autofahrer versuchten, gewaltsam in das Festivalquartier einzudringen bzw. die Wachleute an den Kontrollpunkten anschrieen oder sie anpöbelten.

A Strategy for a Neighborhood without Cars

- Every fifteen minutes, six shuttle buses moved residents between the neighborhood and four temporary parking lots
- A twenty-four-hour support service carried residents with urgent or special needs via electric shuttles upon request
- 400 vehicles (bicycles, electric scooters, electric bikes, and children's trailers) were distributed free of charge to residents for the entire month
- Mail and parcels were delivered by electric vehicles
- Police used light electric vehicles to patrol the neighborhood
- For the amusement of visitors, a bicycle bus, Italian four-wheeled beach bicycles, other EcoMobility vehicles, as well as bicycles were provided at rental stations at all of the entrances to the festival area.

Ein Plan für ein Stadtquartier ohne Autos

- Alle 15 Minuten fuhren sechs Pendelbusse die Bewohner zwischen dem Quartier und vier zeitweisen Parkplätzen hin und her.
- Ein 24-Stunden-Unterstützungsdienst fuhr Bewohner mit dringenden oder speziellen Bedürfnissen bei Bedarf mit Elektro-Pendelfahrzeugen.
- 400 Fahrzeuge (Fahrräder, Elektroroller, e-Bikes und Kinderanhänger) wurden den ganzen Monat über kostenlos an Bewohner verliehen.
- Briefe und Pakete wurden mit Elektrofahrzeugen befördert.
- Die Polizei patrouillierte mit kleinen elektrischen Stehmobilen durch das Quartier.
- Zum ökomobilen Vergnügen der Besucher standen ein Fahrradbus, italienische vierrädrige Strandfahrräder, andere EcoMobility-Fahrzeuge sowie Fahrräder an Verleihstationen an allen Eingängen zum Festivalgelände zur Verfügung.

△
2012

△
September 2013

Suwon's EcoMobility Street

One of the most disputed elements of the rearrangement of Haenggung-dong streets was Jeongjo-ro, the four-lane commercial street bordering the festival area. It is one of Suwon's busiest streets, with an astounding frequency of buses.

The Creative Director of the Festival proposed that Jeongjo-ro could become Suwon's symbolic "EcoMobility Street"—dedicated solely to pedestrians, bicycles, all sorts of other EcoMobility vehicles, as well as buses and taxis. The city pursued this plan seriously, but encountered fierce resistance from the 200 shop owners along the street.

As a comprise, Jeongjo-ro was blocked from cars and trucks for only eight days, and the Suwon EcoMobility Street was arranged with temporary signage and plant containers. Two arches at the entrances to the festival area showed how the meaning of EcoMobility was translated into a new allocation of street space: sidewalks, two lanes for buses and taxis, and the remaining two lanes for bidirectional EcoMobility traffic.

Suwons EcoMobility-Straße

Eines der umstrittensten Elemente bei der Neuordnung der Straßen in Haenggung-dong war die Jeongjo-Straße, die vierspurige Geschäftsstraße, welche die Grenze des Festivalareas bildet. Sie ist eine der geschäftigsten Straßen Suwons mit einer erstaunlichen Busverkehrsfrequenz.

Der Kreativdirektor des Festivals schlug vor, dass die Jeongjo-Straße Suwons symbolische „EcoMobility Street" werden könnte, gewidmet ausschließlich den Fußgängern, Fahrrädern, allen möglichen Arten von EcoMobility-Fahrzeugen sowie Bussen und Taxis. Die Stadt verfolgte diesen Plan ernsthaft, erntete aber erbitterten Widerstand der 200 Ladenbesitzer an der Straße.

Als ein Kompromiss wurde die Jeongjo-Straße für nur acht Tage für Autos und Lastwagen gesperrt und die Suwoner EcoMobility-Straße wurde mit temporärer Beschilderung und Pflanztrögen eingerichtet. Zwei Torbögen an beiden Einfahrten zum Festivalgebiet zeigten, wie die Bedeutung von Ökomobilität in eine neue Aufteilung des Straßenraumes umgesetzt wurde: Gehsteige, zwei Spuren für Busse und Taxis, die verbleibenden zwei Spuren für Ökomobilitätsverkehr in beiden Richtungen.

A Solution to a Problem

Most residents and business people wanted to experience car-free life. The idea of the festival was convincing and evoked curiosity. However, managing without cars in the neighborhood was not always an easy task. But those who encountered problems searched for and found solutions.

Lösung für ein Problem

Autofreies Leben erproben, das wollten die meisten Bewohner und Gewerbetreibenden. Die Idee des Festivals überzeugte und machte neugierig. Der Verzicht auf Kraftfahrzeuge im Quartier war jedoch nicht immer leicht zu meistern. Aber wer ein Problem hatte, suchte und fand eine Lösung.

" Because of the festival I learned how to bike. "

" Wegen des Festivals habe ich das Radfahren erlernt. "

Learning to Cycle

The festival was announced, the citizens enthusiastic about the prospect of an ecomobile lifestyle on car-free streets—but then, many residents had never ridden a bike. Therefore, a bike school was established so that all residents could enjoy riding a bicycle through their quarter.

Radfahren lernen

Das Festival war angekündigt, die Bürger begeistert über die Aussicht eines ökomobilen Lebensstils auf autofreien Straßen – aber dann stellte sich heraus, dass viele Bewohner noch niemals Fahrrad gefahren waren. Deshalb wurde eine Fahrradschule eingerichtet, damit alle Bewohner es genießen konnten, mit dem Fahrrad durch ihr Quartier zu fahren.

" There are people who need a car for deliveries and this is a problem. For example, I contacted my supplier yesterday to tell him that he could not park in front of my restaurant. So I asked him to leave the goods at a friend's store outside the neighborhood. I walked to her store in the morning and picked up the goods. "

Hee Jin Jung, snack bar owner

" Da gibt es Leute, die brauchen ein Auto für Lieferfahrten und das ist ein Problem. Gestern beispielsweise rief ich meinen Lieferanten an und sagte ihm, dass er nicht vor meinem Restaurant halten könne. So bat ich ihn, die Waren im Laden einer Freundin außerhalb des Quartiers abzuliefern. Ich ging dann morgens zu ihrem Laden und holte die Sachen ab. "

Hee Jin Jung, Besitzerin eines Imbissstands

❝ The four months before the festival started, I could not open the shop because construction was going on everywhere. That time was painful. But now I benefit from the improvement, so I am thankful to the residents and planners, who put so much effort into this project.

To have no cars in this neighborhood is the most important and valuable aspect of the festival. Visitors should come and experience how it is. Being here for just one day without cars, I feel so fresh. It feels so different compared to the past. For children, it is good to experience their neighborhood without cars. They learn about the nature and environment through this 'lively visual lesson.'

I personally hope that the culture of EcoMobility will spread out from this neighborhood. I want to encourage international and national politicians to share the ideas of alternative transportation, so that all the nations and all the citizens become more aware of it. **❞**

Hee Jin Jung, snack bar owner

❞ Während der vier Monate vor dem Festivalbeginn konnte ich mein Geschäft nicht öffnen, weil überall Bauarbeiten am Gange waren. Diese Zeit war schmerzhaft. Aber jetzt profitiere ich von der Verbesserung, nun bin ich den Bewohnern und Planern dankbar, die sich soviel Mühe mit dem Projekt gegeben haben.

Im Quartier keine Autos mehr zu haben, ist der wichtigste und wertvollste Aspekt am Festival. Wenn ich hier nur einen Tag ohne Autos verbringe, fühle ich mich so erfrischt. Es fühlt sich so anders als früher an. Für die Kinder ist es gut, ihr Quartier einmal ohne Autos zu erleben. Für sie ist das lebendiger Anschauungsunterricht zu Natur und Umwelt.

Ich persönlich hoffe, dass die Kultur der Ökomobilität sich von diesem Quartier aus verbreiten wird. Ich möchte internationale und nationale Politiker dazu ermutigen, die Ideen zu alternativem Verkehr weiterzugeben, sodass alle Länder und alle Bürger sich dessen mehr bewusst werden. **❝**

Hee Jin Jung, Besitzerin eines Imbissstands

▽
2012

▽
September 2013

The Haenggung-dong Festival Currency

Suwon City was concerned that shops and restaurants in the neighborhood should profit from the festival—as compensation for their support of a car-free neighborhood, which customers could not approach by car. Suwon found a creative solution: cooperating businesses were designated "Festival Member Shop" and could be recognized through a special sign. Coupons as a local, Haenggung-dong Festival currency were introduced.

Suwon City printed coupons in the values of 1,000 and 5,000 Korean Won (0.70 and 3.50 Euros). Festival visitors could purchase coupons, which served as cash to pay for food, bike rentals, vehicle test rides, and other items. Visitors who bought festival currency of more than 10,000 Won received a free coupon for trial programs. Visitors were informed about the local currency through banners and signs.

Coupons were accepted by 195 of the 279 businesses in the neighborhood. The Haenggung-dong currency channeled customers to these cooperating shops. The turnover of coupons during the Festival period amounted to 190 million Won (135,000 Euros)—money that flowed into the tills of local businesses.

Die Festivalwährung von Haenggung-dong

Die Stadt Suwon war darauf bedacht, dass die Geschäfte und Restaurants im Quartier vom Festival profitieren sollten – als Ausgleich für ihre Unterstützung eines autofreien Gebietes, in dem Kunden nicht mehr mit dem Auto bis an die Geschäfte würden heranfahren können. Suwon fand eine kreative Lösung: kooperierende Betriebe wurden zu „Festival-Mitgliedsbetrieben" ernannt, die durch ein spezielles Schild erkennbar waren. Coupons als örtliche Festivalwährung wurden eingeführt.

Die Stadt Suwon druckte Coupons in den Werten 1000 und 5000 koreanische Won (0,70 bzw. 3,50 Euro). Festivalbesucher konnten Coupons erwerben, um Essen, Leihfahrräder, Probefahrten mit Fahrzeugen und andere Dinge zu bezahlen. Besucher, die Coupons im Gegenwert von über 10.000 Won kauften, erhielten einen Freicoupon für die Teilnahme an einem Probefahrtprogramm. Besucher wurden auf Bannern und Schildern über die örtliche Währung informiert. Die Coupons wurden von 195 der 279 Betriebe im Quartier angenommen. Die Währung von Haenggung-dong führte den teilnehmenden Geschäften Kunden zu.

Der Coupon-Umsatz während des Festivalzeitraums erreichte 190 Millionen Won (135.000 Euro), Geld, das in die Kassen der Betriebe floss.

Happiness Unleashed—
The Ecomobile Community
Entfesseltes Glücksgefühl –
die ökomobile Einwohnerschaft

As 1,500 cars disappeared from the streets, much urban space opened up, inviting all sorts of social and cultural activities.

It was indeed fascinating to see people seizing the street space. Coffee shops and bars placed tables and chairs on the sidewalks, allowing people to enjoy fresh air, watch the new street life, and communicate with others across the street. Couples strolled hand in hand along the streets. Families walked with their babies and children in a relaxed way, without being scared by cars. Happiness spread out throughout the neighborhood.

Now the streets were for all. Social life unfolded, which had previously been suppressed by parked automobiles and traffic.

Haenggung-dong residents were proud to be host to so many visitors from all over Korea and abroad.

Nachdem 1500 Autos von den Straßen verschwunden waren, öffnete sich ein umfassender öffentlicher Raum, der zu zahllosen sozialen und kulturellen Aktivitäten einlud.

Es war in der Tat faszinierend zu sehen, wie die Leute den Straßenraum in Besitz nahmen. Cafés und Bars stellten Tische und Stühle auf die Gehwege, damit die Leute die frische Luft genießen, das neue Straßenleben beobachten und mit anderen quer über die Straße kommunizieren konnten. Paare flanierten Hand in Hand die Straßen entlang. Familien gingen mit ihren Babies und Kindern ohne Angst vor Autos spazieren. Fröhlichkeit verbreitete sich im Stadtquartier.

Jetzt waren die Straßen für alle da. Es entfaltete sich soziales Leben, das zuvor durch parkende Autos und Verkehr unterdrückt war.

Die Bewohner von Haenggung-dong waren stolz, so viele Besucher aus ganz Korea und Übersee zu Gast zu haben.

△
2012

▽
September 2013

△▽
September 2013

Easier Work

People didn't just enjoy the ecomobile public space in their leisure time. Hard-working people did, too. Car-free streets eased their strenuous lives.

Erleichterte Arbeit

Nicht nur in ihrer Freizeit genossen Leute die ökomobilen Freiräume. Hart arbeitende Menschen taten es ebenso. Autofreie Straßen erleichterten ihr anstrengendes Leben.

Hilarity Day and Night

It was amazing to watch people in car-free Haenggung-dong. Whether during the day, in the evening, or at night—people enjoyed the space and safety that the EcoMobility World Festival has endowed the neighborhood with.

Fröhlichkeit bei Tag und Nacht

Es war verblüffend, den Menschen im autofreien Haenggung-dong zuzuschauen. Ob tagsüber, abends oder nachts – die Leute genossen den Raum und die Sicherheit, die das EcoMobility World Festival dem Quartier geschenkt hatte.

In Praise of the Festival—Reportage from the Site

"It feels really comfortable to be able to walk the streets and not have any cars. It is difficult to imagine that once there were actually cars in those streets." These words of a visitor express the feelings of many who stroll around the neighborhood during the festival and enjoy the space that was previously dominated by cars.

Asked what they like most about the festival, residents and visitors alike emphatically highlight the sensitive urban renewal and improved appearance of the Haenggung-dong neighborhood—for example, the new design of the streets and storefronts. But most also state that a real increase of quality of living is due to the absence of cars—no noise, no pollution, as well as increased comfort and safety from moving in an ecomobile fashion. Especially parents and their children are experiencing a relaxed time. Also, elderly residents enjoy moving in the streets safely.

Many residents say that they meet more often with friends and neighbors in public space since the Festival started—hence, the changes seem to have an immense effect on community life.

Although frequent car users initially find it difficult to abandon their cars, after a few festival days, they realize that the benefits compensate for any discomfort, and the change of mobility habits is an enriching experience. Businesses also benefit as a result of the many visitors pouring into the neighborhood on weekends.

International guests express their admiration for what the city and the residents have achieved and consider the festival an inspiring experience.

Lob des Festivals – Reportage vom Ortsgeschehen

„Es ist einem angenehm zumute, wenn man auf den Straßen laufen kann, ohne dass es Autos gibt. Es fällt schwer sich vorzustellen, dass auf diesen Straßen mal Autos waren." Diese Worte eines Besuchers stehen für die Eindrücke vieler, die während des Festivals im Quartier herumbummeln und den Raum genießen, der zuvor von Autos dominiert war.

Danach befragt, was sie am Festival am meisten schätzen, heben Bewohner und Besucher gleichermaßen die behutsame Stadterneuerung und das bessere Erscheinungsbild des Quartiers Haenggung-dong hervor, zum Beispiel die neue Straßengestaltung und die Ladenfronten. Aber die meisten sagen auch, dass die wirkliche Erhöhung der Lebensqualität auf der Abwesenheit der Autos beruht – kein Lärm, keine Luftverschmutzung, dafür erhöhte Behaglichkeit und Sicherheit durch die ökomobile Fortbewegung. insbesondere Eltern und ihre Kinder erleben eine entspannte Atmosphäre. Auch ältere Einwohner genießen es, sich auf den Straßen sicher bewegen zu können.

Viele Bewohner sagen, dass sie sich seit dem Festivalbeginn häufiger mit Freunden und Nachbarn im öffentlichen Raum treffen – die Veränderungen wirken sich also auch auf das Gemeinschaftsleben aus.

Obwohl intensive Autonutzer es zuerst schwierig finden, auf ihr Auto zu verzichten, bemerken sie nach einigen Festivaltagen, dass die Vorteile die Unbequemlichkeiten aufwiegen und dass die Änderung der Mobilitätsgewohnheiten eine bereichernde Erfahrung ist. Geschäfte profitieren ebenfalls durch die vielen Besucher, die an Wochenenden in das Quartier strömen.

Internationale Gäste drücken ihre Bewunderung darüber aus, was die Stadt und die Bürger auf die Beine gestellt haben und bewerten das Festival als inspirierende Erfahrung.

Worries and Issues—Reportage from the Site

While most residents are enthusiastic about the festival, we also wanted to learn about their worries and issues.

Now, Haenggung-dong shines in new splendor, but many residents had difficulties with the four-month construction period.

Some shop owners claim they have incurred losses and are concerned that the festival will not compensate for these. Residents who live and work in the side streets are disappointed that the city has not refurbished these, and doubt that it will be done after the festival. Citizens from other Suwon neighborhoods are not happy that only Haenggung-dong has been improved, while other neighborhoods have been neglected.

Many residents and business owners feel that the city could support them better in managing an ecomobile life. Several older and physically impaired residents complain that the alternative shuttle service was not well organized in the first days of the festival. Business owners also reported that initially the supply and delivery of goods by alternative means did not run smoothly.

While Haenggung-dong has been freed from cars, the adjacent neighborhood is burdened by additional vehicles. Particularly in the first festival week—when the main street, Jeongjo-ro, was closed—residents in nearby areas were annoyed by the redirected traffic and parked vehicles.

Others criticize the top-down manner of the festival organization. They feel that the planning and preparation process was not sufficiently transparent and that the residents were not consulted adequately. Some feel that the festival program mainly focuses on the visitors, and not on the residents. In their opinion, the festival makes daily life more complicated, especially for car commuters and business owners. They express the wish that the festival would be shorter, opting for smaller steps towards the adaptation of ecomobile lifestyles.

Sorgen und Probleme – Reportage vom Ortsgeschehen

Die meisten Bewohner waren zwar vom Festival begeistert; aber wir wollten auch ihre Sorgen und Probleme verstehen.

Heute erscheint Haenggung-dong in neuem Glanz, aber viele Bewohner hatten mit der viermonatigen Bauphase Probleme.

Einige Ladeninhaber geben an, Verluste hinnehmen zu müssen, und haben Sorge, dass das Festival diese nicht ausgleichen wird. Bewohner, die in den Seitenstraßen leben und arbeiten, sind enttäuscht, dass die Stadt nicht auch diese saniert hat, und bezweifeln, dass dies nach dem Festival erfolgen wird. Einwohner aus anderen Stadtteilen Suwons sind nicht glücklich darüber, dass nur Haenggung-dong aufgebessert wurde, während andere Quartiere vernachlässigt würden.

Viele Bewohner und Geschäftsleute meinen, die Stadt könne sie besser dabei unterstützen, den ökomobilen Lebensstil zu handhaben. Einige ältere und körperbehinderte Bewohner beschweren sich darüber, dass der alternative Shuttledienst in den ersten Festivaltagen nicht gut organisiert gewesen sei. Auch berichten Geschäftsleute, dass anfangs die Versorgung mit und Auslieferung von Waren auf alternative Weise nicht glatt lief.

Während Haenggung-dong von Autos befreit ist, wird das angrenzende Quartier mit zusätzlichen Fahrzeugen belastet. Besonders in der ersten Festivalwoche, als die Hauptstraße Jeongjo-ro geschlossen war, fühlten sich Bewohner in nahegelegenen Gebieten durch den umgeleiteten Verkehr und parkende Autos belästigt.

Andere kritisieren die Organisation des Festivals von oben herab. Sie meinen, dass der Planungs- und Vorbereitungsprozess nicht ausreichend transparent gewesen sei und die Bewohner nicht angemessen konsultiert worden seien. Einige meinen, dass das Festivalprogramm sich überwiegend an Besucher, nicht an die Bürger richte. Ihrer Meinung nach erschwert das Festival das tägliche Leben, besonders für Autopendler und Geschäftsleute. Sie drücken den Wunsch aus, das Festival möge kürzer sein und bevorzugen kleinere Schritte in Richtung auf ökomobile Lebensstile.

Young Koreans on EcoMobility—Reportage from the Site

There is no need to persuade Young-Ja Lim about the advantages of Eco-Mobility, as she already lives an ecomobile life. "I could not be happier than now. No cars, no smell, no noise—this is how older people want to live," she explains. But if it is good for the elderly, why is it so difficult for the young generation? "For them, it is hard to live without a car. Life is just too busy."

"Young people get accustomed to the comforts of a car at an early stage in life," argues Chang Yong Ko, who is in his twenties and owns a café in the neighborhood. He thinks that the parents are to blame: "The children get a ride whenever they want. This is spoiling them completely; they cannot even imagine a life without cars." But he also admits that life of a high school student is tough nowadays. The ride from their parents allows them to commute between school and private lessons and to manage their daily schedule.

So how can young adults switch to the ecomobile lifestyle instead? "They need to make firsthand experience," suggests Seng-Jin Ryu, another young resident. "Therefore, the festival should particularly address this age group by offering something like a 'monastery experience': they should be allowed to move in here for a week and live like a local resident. Then they will realize how easy and comfortable it is to live without cars."

Junge Koreaner über Ökomobilität – Reportage vom Ortsgeschehen

Man braucht Young-Ja Lim nicht von den Vorzügen der Ökomobilität zu überzeugen. Denn sie lebt bereits einen ökomobilen Lebensstil. „Ich könnte nicht glücklicher sein als jetzt. Keine Autos, kein Gestank, kein Lärm – so möchten die Älteren leben", sagt sie. Aber wenn dies für die Älteren gut ist, warum ist es für die junge Generation so schwierig? „Für die ist es schlimm, ohne Auto zu leben. Das Leben ist einfach zu hektisch."

„Junge Leute werden schon früh an die Annehmlichkeiten des Autos gewöhnt", sagt Chang-Yong Ko, der in den Zwanzigern ist und ein Café im Quartier besitzt. Er findet, dass die Eltern schuld sind: „Die Kinder werden mit dem Auto chauffiert, wann immer sie wollen. Das verwöhnt sie total; sie können sich ein Leben ohne Autos nicht einmal mehr vorstellen." Aber er gibt auch zu, dass das Leben eines Schülers heute hart ist. Die Fahrt mit den Eltern erlaubt es ihnen, zwischen Schule und Privatstunden zu pendeln und das Tagesprogramm zu meistern.

Wie können also junge Erwachsene stattdessen auf einen ökomobilen Lebensstil umschalten? „Sie müssen eigene Erfahrungen machen", schlägt Seng-Jin Ryu, ein anderer junger Bewohner, vor. „Deshalb sollte das Festival speziell diese Altersgruppe ansprechen, indem es so etwas wie eine ‚Kloster-Erfahrung' vermittelt. Sie sollten für eine Woche hier einziehen können und wie ein Bewohner leben. Dann werden sie merken, wie leicht und bequem es ist, ohne Auto zu leben."

▽
2012

▽
September 2013

" So many people visit the area in these days! **"**

" So viele Leute besuchen das Gebiet in diesen Tagen! **"**

" For my daughter, the walk to school is safer now. **"**

" Der Schulweg ist für meine Tochter sicherer geworden. **"**

" The Festival is good for cohesion of the neighborhood. **"**

" Das Festival ist gut für den Zusammenhalt des Stadtquartiers. **"**

" The festival is good for my business. **"**

" Das Festival ist gut für mein Geschäft. **"**

" The festival creates a lively atmosphere. **"**

" Das Festival schafft eine lebendige Atmosphäre. **"**

" Air pollution has definitely decreased. **"**

" Die Luftverschmutzung ist definitiv gesunken. **"**

Comprehensive Visual Identity

The corporate design of the EcoMobility World Festival was consistently applied throughout the neighborhood. From program brochures to newsletters, from flags to banners, from bus schedules to parking licenses, from restaurant menus to public toilets, from calendars to notebooks, stickers, postcards, business cards—all communication products featured the EcoMobility Festival's visual identity. Even comic figures were developed for the festival and especially enjoyed by kids.

Two logos were created—one for international use and one for local purposes. The visual identity fell somewhat apart.

Communication was nevertheless powerful. Locally as well as internationally, this first festival of its kind gained a high level of recognition through the consistent use of the corporate design.

Umfassende visuelle Identität

Das Erscheinungsbild des EcoMobility World Festivals wurde im gesamten Stadtquartier durchgängig gestaltet. Von der Programmbroschüre bis zu Newslettern, von Flaggen bis zu Bannern, von Busfahrplänen bis zu Parkplaketten, von Restaurant-Speisekarten bis zu öffentlichen Toiletten, von Kalendern bis zu Notizbüchern, Aufklebern, Postkarten, Visitenkarten – alle Kommunikationsprodukte zeigten die visuelle Identität des Festivals. Sogar Comicfiguren wurden speziell für das Festival entwickelt und erfreuten vor allem Kinder.

Zwei Logos wurden geschaffen – eines für internationalen Gebrauch, das andere für örtliche Zwecke. Die visuelle Identität fiel ein wenig auseinander.

Die Kommunikation war dennoch wirksam. Sowohl vor Ort als auch im internationalen Bereich gewann dieses erste Festival seiner Art hohe Beachtung aufgrund der durchgehenden Anwendung des Corporate Designs.

◁
Flags along the EcoMobility Street
Beflaggung entlang der EcoMobility-Straße

◁▽
Mobile public toilets in festival look
Toilettenwagen im Festival-Look

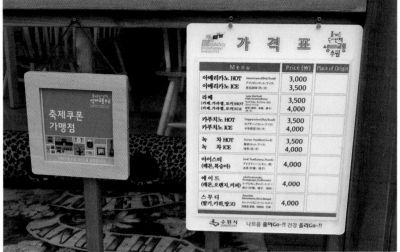

Restaurants attracted guests with special festival menus in English, and served meals on festival place settings. The blue signs indicated that festival currency was accepted.
Restaurants zogen Besucher mit speziellen Speisekarten in Englisch an und servierten auf Festival-Platzdecken. Das blaue Schild zeigte an, dass die Festival-Währung akzeptiert wird.

어수선하던 거리가 이렇게

변화 전 (Before) 변화 중 (Middle) 변화 후 (After)

Information tableaus throughout Haenggung-dong showed the images of a street or square in its earlier state, during the construction period, and its new appearance after completion.
Informationstafeln im gesamten Quartier zeigten Bilder einer Straße oder eines Platzes im ursprünglichen Zustand, während der Umbauphase sowie in neuer Erscheinung nach der Fertigstellung.

International Media Outreach
Internationale Medienarbeit

The Festival idea was conveyed to **1,000** member cities in **86** countries representing **500** million inhabitants

122 articles from **85** international media outlets (Reuters, Deutsche Welle, Monocle, Global Urbanist) were published, with another **185** articles in the Korean press

44 blog entries were published, generating **3,673** page views from **95** countries

Out of the **25,000** photos taken **364** were uploaded to flickr generating **8,519** views

4 international documentaries and **12** local videos plus **35** video contest contributions have been produced

5 YouTube videos generated **1,600** views

Documentaries posted on Vimeo targeted at an expert audience counted over **150** views

A daily newsletter was sent out to **82,333** email accounts with opening rates of **22%**

△
ICLEI's Head of Global Communications, Katrina Borromeo, being given a lift by EcoMobility Team Leader Santhosh Kodukula
ICLEIs internationale Kommunikationschefin Katrina Borromeo, chauffiert von EcoMobility-Teamleiter Santhosh Kodukula

❝ Check out any news about transport, and you'll find that it's mostly limited to frenzied road mishaps and gruesome traffic accidents. This makes the idea of the EcoMobility World Festival, or having one neighborhood go on a month-long, car-free diet a tough sell. To attract media coverage of the festival, we took a unique approach of blending mainstream media with social media, putting transport experts, citizens, and young people at the core of our efforts. ❞

Katrina Borromeo, Head of ICLEI Global Communications

❞ Schau Nachrichten über Verkehr an und du wirst feststellen, dass sie überwiegend auf wilde Raserei und schreckliche Verkehrsunfälle beschränkt sind. Dies macht es schwer, die Idee des EcoMobility-Welt-Festivals, ein Stadtquartier für einen Monat auf autofreie Diät zu setzen, medienwirksam zu verkaufen. Um Medienberichte über das Festival zu erzeugen, wählten wir den Ansatz, die traditionellen Medien mit sozialen Medien zu kombinieren, wobei wir Verkehrsexperten, Bürger und junge Leute in den Mittelpunkt unserer Berichterstattung stellten. ❝

Katrina Borromeo, Head of ICLEI Global Communications

Local Media Outreach
Örtliche Medienarbeit

Haenggung-dong in the Spotlight
Newspaper, radio, and TV reporters from Korea, China, Japan, and elsewhere flocked to Suwon to cover the unique mise en scène of an ecomobile neighborhood. They recorded the grand opening ceremony, the VIP parade and Mayors' Ride, the EcoMobility Congress, the multitude of conferences and cultural events, and most importantly, the happy street life in car-free Haenggung-dong.

Haenggung-dong im Rampenlicht
Zeitungs-, Radio- und Fernsehreporter strömten nach Suwon, um über die einzigartige Inszenierung eines ökomobilen Stadtquartiers zu berichten. Sie berichteten über die großartige Eröffnungszeremonie, die VIP-Parade, die Bürgermeistertour, den EcoMobility-Kongress, die Vielzahl von Tagungen und Kulturereignissen und vor allem über das fröhliche Straßenleben im autofreien Haenggung-dong.

Public Relations in the Neighborhood
Extensive awareness raising, education, and information were key components of the festival process. Newsletters informed the residents of Haenggung-dong about the upcoming festival and preparatory activities by the citizens.

Öffentlichkeitsarbeit im Quartier
Umfassende Aufklärung, Schulung und Information waren Kernkomponenten des Festivalprozesses. Mitteilungsblätter informierten die Bewohner Haenggung-dongs über das bevorstehende Festival und die Vorbereitungsarbeiten der Bürger.

350 tweets
300 followers
400 facebook posts
360 likes
262 blogs
87,000 visits
11,000 posters
15,000 folded leaflets
55,000 festival brochures

다녀왔어요!

편지리 쓰고 돌잡소녀같은 어머님들

몇십년 만에 동네 친구들과의 외출이다. 이런 기회를 만들어 준 진행부에 감사한다. 신풍동에 사는 정말 행복하다. 생태교통이 성공적으로 치뤄지길 기대한다 -박명희님

편안하고 가족적인 분위기에 너무 좋았다 -봉근식

정말 기분이 좋다 감사하다. 이런 기회가 또 있었으면 좋겠다 -주후숙님

우리를 도와주시고 고맙습니다 -장안 경로당 동네사람들과 나오니까 좋습니다 -이승익님 자전거 배우면서 생태교통축제에 대한 기대가 더 커졌습니다 -이해영님

여행 좋아하는데 부부동반 해서 갈일이 별로 없었는데 동네행사로 부부반 같이 가니 더 좋았다 -정영희님

언제 갈지 기다려지고 행복하고 즐거웠다 -차인순

정겹고 소박한 건배도 해보고!

음이 아까 말설이다가 4개월 만에 소풍을 나왔는데 날씨도 좋고 기분도 전환되고 너무 감사하고 고맙다. 남편이 걱정이 되는지 1시간 마다 안부 전화를 한다. 참으로 고맙고 행복한 하루였다 -김원숙님

해미 읍성에서 세그웨이도 타며 즐거웠잖!

혼자갔다는 동 동네분들이 가족같이 대해줘서 불볼합없이 답사 잘하고 돌아왔다 -민희진님

2013년 9월 생태교통의 달에 우리동네를 돌아 다닐 '세그웨이' (입명·왕발통)도 함께 다녀왔습니다. 생태교통 참여 주민들은 5월13일 (월)부터 나네주민안내소에 미리 예약하면 누구든지 체험 할 수 있습니다. (단 중학생 이상만 신청가능)

협찬해 주셔서 감사합니다
팔달구청장, 행궁동주민자치위원회, 신풍동 30통장
생태교통주민추진단(단장),부단장,상가경제분과장,홍보분과장,주민고충분과장,글로벌녹색스분과사무1

Documentaries Ensure Lasting Impressions

The festival has been extensively documented. Photographers, filmmakers, interviewers, and reporters were engaged by Suwon City and ICLEI, and tasked with capturing the process and its outcomes in words, images, and sounds. Besides the EcoMobility Festival website, a Festival Report, a Congress Report, and several film documentaries have been produced.

Reportagen sorgen für bleibende Eindrücke

Das Festival ist ausführlich dokumentiert worden. Fotografen, Filmer, Interviewer und Berichterstatter wurden von der Stadt Suwon und ICLEI engagiert, um den Prozess und seine Ergebnisse in Wort, Bild und Ton festzuhalten.
Neben der Webseite zum EcoMobility Festival sind ein Festivalbericht, ein Kongressbericht sowie mehrere Dokumentarfilme hergestellt worden.

△
The film team of The Urban Idea & Fietscher Film in action: Daniel Huhn, Theresa Zimmermann
Das Filmteam von The Urban Idea & Fietscher Film bei der Arbeit: Daniel Huhn, Theresa Zimmermann

◁
Interviewer Tobias Kuttler (in white shirt) and his Korean translator speaking with a visitor
Interviewer Tobias Kuttler (im weißen Hemd) und sein koreanischer Übersetzer im Gespräch mit einer Besucherin

Videos and more information
Videos und weitere Informationen

http://www.theurbanidea.com/festivalfilms.html
http://www.theurbanidea.com/festivalreport.html
http://www.theurbanidea.com/congressreport.html

The streets of Suwon - 30 min
von The Urban Idea GmbH

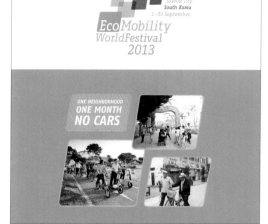

A city goes ecomobile - 16 min
von The Urban Idea GmbH

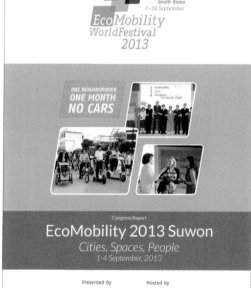

Showing the future today - 11 min
von The Urban Idea GmbH

The key feature of the festival project was that it was a mise en scène of future urban ecomobile life. Residents would remove their cars from the area and experience an ecomobile lifestyle.

This required that a variety of EcoMobility vehicles be provided to residents and visitors.

Das Wesensmerkmal des Festivalprojekts war die Inszenierung eines zukünftigen ökomobilen Stadtlebens. Bürger würden ihre Autos aus dem Gebiet entfernen und einen ökomobilen Lebensstil erfahren.

Dies erforderte, dass den Bewohnern und Besuchern eine Vielfalt an Ökomobilitätsfahrzeugen zur Verfügung gestellt würde.

Acquisition of EcoMobility Vehicles

Suwon City purchased over 400 bicycles and gave them to the residents who wished to use a bike as replacement for their car, as well as 300 bicycles for its rental stations around the festival area.

ICLEI approached companies worldwide inviting them to provide vehicles to the festival. Eighteen international companies from ten countries provided eighty different kinds of rare and innovative ecomobile vehicles catering to a wide range of mobility needs—including LEVs (Light Electric Vehicles) that are fun and exciting to ride, multiperson vehicles, as well as exercise-oriented vehicles. Some of these models were not yet known or available in South Korea or elsewhere in Asia.

Yellow Bike—a Suwon-based, social enterprise—was entrusted with the assembly and maintenance of the EcoMobility vehicles that were provided to residents, rented out to visitors, and shown in the exhibition.

Beschaffung von EcoMobility-Fahrzeugen

Die Stadt Suwon beschaffte über 400 Fahrräder und stellte sie den Einwohnern zur Verfügung, die ein Fahrrad als Ersatz für ihr Auto haben wollten. Sie kaufte auch 300 Fahrräder für die Verleihstationen rund um das Festivalareal.

ICLEI wandte sich an Hersteller weltweit und lud sie dazu ein, Fahrzeuge für das Festival zur Verfügung zu stellen. 18 internationale Hersteller aus zehn Ländern brachten 80 verschiedene Typen von seltenen und innovativen Fahrzeugen für eine breite Palette von Mobilitätsanforderungen ein, von leichten Elektrofahrzeugen (LEVs) die beim Fahren begeistern und Spaß bereiten, über Mehrpersonenfahrzeuge bis hin zu Fahrzeugen für körperliches Training. Einige dieser Modelle waren in Korea und teilweise in ganz Asien noch nicht bekannt oder verfügbar.

Das in Suwon ansässige gemeinnützige Unternehmen Yellow Bike wurde mit der Montage und Wartung von Ökomobilitätsfahrzeugen betraut, die Bewohnern zur Verfügung gestellt, an Besucher verliehen und in der Ausstellung gezeigt wurden.

◁
Tazo by Tazorider;
kickTrike by Greenpack;
Virto by M-Products

△
Trimobil by Toxy Liegerad

△
Velotaxi from China

△
Row-n-Go bike by Row-n-go

◁
Zigo Leader X1
Carrier Bicycle

When talking to international companies about contributing ecomobile vehicles to the world's first EcoMobility World Festival, the most common reaction was curiosity about the project, surprise regarding the location, and often skepticism regarding the time frame. The barriers to involvement that we heard about were mainly 'no budget' (or already allocated), dependency on local distributors' involvement (who often turned out to be uninterested), the unavailability of vehicles during the relevant period, or the inability to recognize the immense potential of this global advertising opportunity.

Eighteen daring companies, however, took that leap of faith and contributed eighty vehicles for the festival. These ranged from innovative light electric vehicles to practical trailers. In the end, two-thirds of the vehicles were donated to Suwon City for continuous support of EcoMobility efforts.

Mona Ludigkeit, Business Liaison EcoMobility World Festival 2013

◁
Virto by
M-Products

Als wir mit internationalen Unternehmen darüber sprachen, ökomobile Fahrzeuge zum weltersten EcoMobility World Festival beizusteuern, waren die üblichsten Reaktionen: Neugier nach dem Projekt, Überraschung über den Ort und oft Skepsis bezüglich des Zeitrahmens. Die Herausforderungen waren hauptsächlich ‚kein Budget' (oder es war bereits verplant), Abhängigkeit von der Beteiligung des örtlichen Distributeurs, der sich oft uninteressiert zeigte, die Nichtverfügbarkeit von Fahrzeugen in dem betreffenden Zeitraum, oder dass die Firmen das immense Potenzial des Festivals zur weltweiten Werbung nicht erkannten.

18 mutige Unternehmen zeigten jedoch Vertrauensvorschuss und trugen zum Festival mit 80 Fahrzeugen bei, von leichten Elektrofahrzeugen (LEVs) bis zu praktischen Anhängern. Zwei Drittel dieser Fahrzeuge wurden anschließend der Stadt Suwon gespendet.

Mona Ludigkeit, Business Liaison EcoMobility World Festival 2013

▽
Bicycle bus made in Suwon

▽
Pedersen from Manufaktur Kalkhoff

▽
Get1 Ambulance E-bike by gobaX

86

EcoMobility Vehicles Exhibition

Dozens of models of innovative bicycles and light electric vehicles were displayed in the EcoMobility Vehicles Exhibition, for which Suwon City had set up a special pavilion on Haenggung-dong Plaza.

EcoMobility-Fahrzeugausstellung

Dutzende von Modellen innovativer Fahrräder und leichter Elektrofahrzeuge waren in der EcoMobility-Fahrzeugausstellung zu sehen, für die die Stadt Suwon eigens einen Pavillon auf der Haenggung-dong-Plaza aufgestellt hatte.

Cycles
Egretta (Aryen Motor)
Pedersen (Pedersen Manufaktur Kalkhoff)

Recumbent bikes
Origami&Trikon (Azub)
Trimobil (Toxy Liegerad)

Electric bikes
Get1 ambulance bike (gobaX)
iLady E-bike & iSport E-bike (inskey)

Person mobility support
Active Walker & Breeze Walker (Acces Vital)

Light electric vehicles
kickTrike (Greenpack)
MoVi (Tünkers)
Virto (M-products)
YikeBike Fusion & Synergy (YikeBike)

Kids & pets
Pico Kids Trike (Inskey Energy Technology)
MoVi (Tünkers)
All Seacon Cargo Trailer (Nordic Cab)

Shopping & delivery
T1 trailer/Luggage (Free Parable Design)
All Season Cargo Trailer (Nordic Cab)

Fun, sports & leisure
T2 Single-wheel Trailer (Free Parable Design)
All Season Sport 5-in-1 Bike Trailer (Nordic Cab)
Row'n'Go Bike (Rowngo)

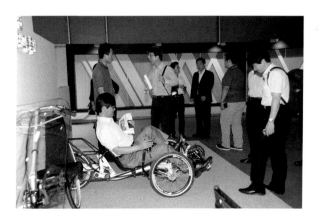

△△
Tricon by Azug and
T1 luggage trailer by FreeParable

△
Trimobil by Toxy Liegerad

◁
MoVi by Tünkers

▽
Monowheel YikeBike by YikeBike

▽
7-seat conference bike

▽
Egretta by Aryen

EcoMobility Parades

On four days, parades presenting a broad range of EcoMobility vehicles took place in the streets of Haenggung-dong, among them a VIP Parade and a Mayors Ride.

EcoMobility-Umzüge

An vier Tagen fanden EcoMobility-Festumzüge statt, bei denen eine breite Palette von EcoMobility-Fahrzeugen präsentiert wurde, darunter eine VIP-Parade und eine Bürgermeistertour.

66 I think that living in a car-centric city is uncomfortable. 99

99 Ich denke, dass es unbequem ist, in einer autozentrierten Stadt zu leben. 66

66 We save the environment and experience the future of mobility. 99

99 Wir schützen die Umwelt und erfahren die Zukunft der Mobilität. 66

66 I'm happy about the free bike rental for one month. 99

99 Ich freue mich über den kostenlosen Fahrradverleih für einen Monat. 66

66 Living here without cars feels so different. 99

99 Hier ohne Auto zu leben, ist so ein anderes Gefühl. 66

66 Changing our mobility habits is a painful process. 99

99 Die Veränderung unserer Mobilitäts-gewohnheiten ist ein schmerzhafter Prozess. 66

66 The culture of EcoMobility will spread out from this neighborhood. 99

99 Die Kultur der Ökomobilität wird sich von diesem Stadtquartier aus verbreiten. 66

2 grand-ceremonies (opening, closing)

13 tours

19 exhibitions

3 other events

6 conferences

4 parades

58 cultural events

7 learning events

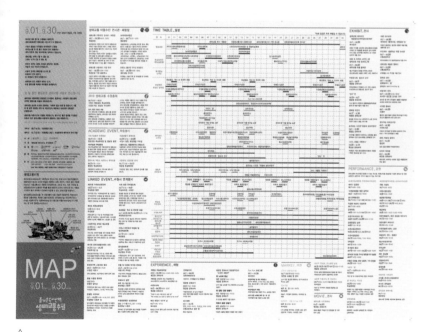

△
A guide map informed visitors about the daily program for the month-long Festival.
Eine Übersichtskarte informierte die Besucher über das Programm an jedem Tag des einmonatigen Festivals.

The Festival of Events

The EcoMobility World Festival was not just a single event. It was a two-year discussion and planning process, and during the month of September 2013, it was a series of more than one hundred events: ceremonies, conferences, parades, tours, exhibitions, learning shows, and cultural performances. There was always something happening for residents and visitors. No wonder that in the end, over one million visits were counted.

All of these events were coordinated, supported, and often conceived and initiated by Suwon City's Festival Team.

Das Festival der Ereignisse

Das EcoMobility World Festival war nicht einfach eine einzige Veranstaltung. Es war ein zwei Jahre dauernder Diskussions- und Planungsprozess und während des Monats September 2013 eine Folge von über 100 Veranstaltungen: Zeremonien, Konferenzen, Umzüge, Touren, Ausstellungen, Lernshows und Kulturereignisse. Für Bürger und Besucher war immer etwas los. Kein Wunder, dass am Ende über eine Million Besuche der verschiedenen Veranstaltungen gezählt wurden.

Alle diese Veranstaltungen wurden durch das Festivalteam der Stadt Suwon koordiniert, unterstützt und nicht selten auch konzipiert und initiiert.

Streets for All

Barrier-free mobility is a particular concern within the concept of EcoMobility. During visually impaired mobility tours and wheelchair mobility tours, visitors had the opportunity to experience streets and alleys under the conditions of disabled people.

Ms. Kyung-sook Han, President of the Disabled Association of Suwon (on the photo in a wheelchair), praised the festival because it provided favorable mobility conditions for the 213 disabled residents of Haenggung-dong. "Only one's own experience can bring about the insight that accessibility is a right," Ms. Han says. "Accessibility is not a special favor to the disabled, but necessary for our communal life."

Straßen für Alle

Barrierefreie Mobilität ist ein besonderes Anliegen im Konzept der Ökomobilität. Im Rahmen von Touren für Blindenmobilität und Rollstuhlmobilität hatten Besucher Gelegenheit, Straßen und Gassen unter den Bedingungen Behinderter zu erleben.

Frau Kyung-sook Han, Vorsitzende des Suwoner Behindertenvereins (auf dem Foto im Rollstuhl), lobte das Festival, weil es angenehme Mobilitätsbedingungen für die 213 Behinderten im Haenggung-dong-Quartier mit sich brachte. „Nur eigene Erfahrung kann die Einsicht hervorbringen, dass Barrierefreiheit ein Recht ist", sagt Frau Han. „Barrierefreiheit ist nicht ein besonderes Entgegenkommen den Behinderten gegenüber, sondern notwendig für unser aller Zusammenleben."

Tours

A variety of tours were organized and offered to both domestic and foreign visitors: King Jeongjo tour, Hwaseong Fortress bicycle tour, village renaissance tour, Suwon tour, Haenggung-dong neighborhood tour, small alley tour, wheelchair tour, visually impaired tour, bicycle bus tour, light electric vehicles (LEV) tour, velotaxi tour, future EcoMobility neighborhood tour, donkey carriage tour … (also see photos on page 94).

Touren

Eine Vielfalt an Touren für koreanische und ausländische Besucher wurden organisiert und angeboten: König-Jeongjo-Gedächtnistour, Fahrradtour entlang der Festung Hwaseong, Suwon-Tour, Haenggung-dong-Quartierstour, Gassentour, Rollstuhltour, Sehbehindertentour, Fahrradbustour, LEV-Tour mit elektrischen Leichtfahrzeugen, Velotaxitour, EcoMobility-Quartierstour, Eselkarrentour, … (siehe auch Fotos auf Seite 94).

Cultural events

The car-free streets of Haenggung-dong offered space for concerts, street theater, dancing performances, fashion shows, King Jeongjo parades, and other cultural delights.

Kulturereignisse

Die autofreien Straßen von Haenggung-dong boten Raum für Konzerte, Straßentheater, Tanzaufführungen, Modeschauen, König-Jeongjo-Paraden und andere kulturelle Vergnügen.

▷
bottom from left to right:
ICLEI Deputy Secretary General Monika Zimmermann, congress participants,
ICLEI EcoMobility Team Leader Santhosh Kodukula
▷
unten von links nach rechts:
ICLEIs Stellv. Generalsekretärin Monika Zimmermann, Kongressteilnehmer,
ICLEIs EcoMobility Teamleiter Santhosh Kodukula

EcoMobility Congress

Over 600 representatives of local governments, non-governmental organizations, international agencies, and companies from forty countries from all continents participated in ICLEI's second EcoMobility World Congress in Suwon. In twenty-four sessions, they discussed transport as the fastest-growing source of climate-damaging emissions, and adopted the *Suwon Impulse*—a guiding document for cities on the pathway to EcoMobility.

EcoMobility-Kongress

Über 600 Vertreter von Kommunen, Verbänden, internationalen Organisationen und Unternehmen aus 40 Ländern von allen Erdteilen nahmen an ICLEIs zweitem EcoMobility-Weltkongress in Suwon teil. In 24 Sitzungen diskutierten sie über den Verkehr als die am rasantesten wachsende Quelle von klimaschädlichen Emissionen und verabschiedeten den Impuls von Suwon – eine Leitlinie für Kommunen auf dem Weg zur ökomobilen Stadt. Das autofreie Quartier war eine lebende Illustration dessen, was in den Sitzungen diskutiert wurde.

◁

Recognition: Festival Creative Director Konrad Otto-Zimmermann, on behalf of the global cities association ICLEI, presenting a plaque of appreciation to Mayor Tae-Young Yeom. He also handed over the EcoMobility vehicles that had been in use during the Festival and were now donated to the city by the manufacturers.
Anerkennung: Der Kreativdirektor des Festivals, Konrad Otto-Zimmermann, überreichte im Namen des Weltstädteverbandes ICLEI eine Würdigungsplakette an Bürgermeister Tae-young Yeom. Er übergab auch EcoMobility-Fahrzeuge, die während des Festivals in Beutzung gewesen waren und nun von den Herstellern der Stadt geschenkt wurden.

△△

Finale: Three thousand citizens watching the closing ceremony on Haenggung-dong Plaza
Finale: 3000 Bürger schauten bei der Schlußzeremonie auf der Haenggung-dong-Plaza zu.

◁

Drinks and tears: the residents of Haenggung-dong celebrate a successful Festival
Drinks und Tränen: die Bewohner Haenggung-dongs feiern ein erfolgreiches Festival.

Good-bye, Festival

As the last evening of the festival drew to a close, its Creative Director made a last tour through the car-free neighborhood. He enjoyed the calm space, quiet atmosphere, and clean air in the streets and alleys. What would the quarter look like tomorrow morning when the cars were back?

Two hours before midnight on September 30, 2013, city officials began removing the barriers at the checkpoints around the Haenggung-dong neighborhood. The gates opened for the invasion.

Auf Wiedersehen, Festival

Am Abend des 30. September unternahm der Kreativdirektor des Festivals eine letzte Tour durch das autofreie Stadtquartier. Er erfreute sich an dem stillen Raum, der ruhigen Atmosphäre und der sauberen Luft in den Straßen und Gassen. Wie würde das Quartier morgen früh aussehen, wenn die Autos zurück wären?

Zwei Stunden vor Mitternacht am 30. September 2013 begannen städtische Mitarbeiter, die Sperren rund um das Stadtquartier Haenggung-dong zu beseitigen. Die Tore öffneten sich für die Invasion.

The Invasion

On the morning of October 1, cars rolled back into what had been a car-free quarter for a month. SUVs reconquered the historic alleys, while sentimental residents sought to hold on to pockets of car-free life.

Die Invasion

Am Morgen des 1. Oktober rollten Autos zurück in das, was einen Monat lang ein autofreies Quartier gewesen war. SUVs eroberten die historischen Gassen zurück, während sentimentale Bewohner Inseln autofreien Lebens festzuhalten versuchten.

Maintaining the Benefits

"Since the festival started, people are walking on the streets freely, with happy faces. But the process towards it was really tough. For four months, there was construction every single day, including much dirt and noise. There were almost no customers then. Now my business is running well again.

Before the festival, many drivers used this neighborhood as a shortcut because there were no traffic lights. This was really annoying. Things have also improved for the children. My three-year-old nephew can now walk safely in the streets. Before, I always had to hold his hand because of the cars.

When I have children on my own, I would like to live in an ecomobile city. EcoMobility is good for the elderly and kids, but those who commute need to use a car every day.

I don't want to go back to the past anymore. We dedicated so much time and effort to prepare the festival; I want it to be the norm and not just for a month. But I do worry that people will start to bring their cars back and that it will be crowded like before. In the future, the cycling infrastructure needs to be improved, here in the neighborhood and in the whole city."

Chang Yong Ko, coffee shop owner

Die Vorteile erhalten

"Seit Beginn des Festivals bewegen sich die Leute frei in den Straßen, mit fröhlichen Gesichtern. Aber der Weg dahin war wirklich hart. Da waren die Bauarbeiten jeden einzelnen Tag über vier Monate hinweg. Da waren so viel Dreck und Lärm. Da hatte ich fast keine Kunden. Aber jetzt läuft mein Geschäft wieder gut.

Vorher haben viele Autofahrer das Quartier als Abkürzung genutzt, weil es keine Ampeln gibt. Das fand ich wirklich ärgerlich. Auch für die Kinder haben sich die Bedingungen verbessert. Vorher musste ich meinen dreijährigen Neffen wegen der Autos ständig an der Hand halten. Aber jetzt kann er sich im Straßenraum sicher bewegen.

Wenn ich mal eigene Kinder habe, würde ich gern in einer ökomobilen Stadt leben. Ökomobilität ist gut für die Älteren und Kinder, aber die Pendler brauchen täglich ihr Auto.

Ich möchte nicht gern in die Vergangenheit zurück. Wir haben der Vorbereitung des Festivals so viel Zeit und Mühe gewidmet; es wäre toll, den Zustand dauerhaft zu erhalten. Aber ich fürchte, dass die Leute ihre Autos zurückbringen und das Gebiet bald so vollgestopft sein wird wie vorher. In Zukunft muss die Infrastruktur für Fahrräder verbessert werden, hier im Stadtquartier wie in der gesamten Stadt."

Chang Yong Ko, Cafébesitzer

Bottom-up, Top-down?

" First I was not in favor of the festival, but in the end this neighborhood became very pretty and friendly for pedestrians. When you walk, you can have a look at all the little things and appreciate them. When you drive a car, you miss a lot of things.

To go beyond the neighborhood, I usually used a car. But during this event, I took the bus. This festival was an eye-opening event; it gave us the opportunity to think about what an alternative future could look like.

The festival could have been more successful if residents had been involved more in the preparations, allowing the idea to become close to their hearts. But I also see the difficulty. When the City Hall announces an event like this, many Koreans just tend to be against it. Maybe more preparation time would not have changed anything. Though it is ironic, knowing the Korean mindset, it was probably the right thing to take up a top-to-bottom approach in organizing the festival. "

Hyun Sil Lee, housewife

Bottom-up, top-down?

" Zuerst war ich nicht für das Festival, aber letztendlich wurde das Quartier sehr hübsch und fußgängerfreundlich. Wenn du läufst, kannst du all die kleinen Dinge sehen und schätzen. Wenn du Auto fährst, verpasst du vieles. Außerhalb des Quartiers habe ich normalerweise ein Auto benutzt. Aber während der vier Wochen bin ich Bus gefahren. Das Festival hat die Augen geöffnet; es hat uns die Gelegenheit gegeben, darüber nachzudenken, wie eine andere Zukunft aussehen könnte.

Das Festival hätte erfolgreicher sein können, wenn die Bewohner mehr in die Vorbereitungen einbezogen gewesen wären; dann hätten sie sich die Idee mehr zu Herzen genommen. Aber ich sehe auch die Schwierigkeit. Wenn die Stadtverwaltung ein Projekt wie dieses ankündigt, sind viele Koreaner erst einmal dagegen. Vielleicht hätte eine längere Vorbereitungszeit daran nichts geändert. Obwohl es ironisch ist, wenn man die koreanische Einstellung kennt, war es vielleicht der richtige Ansatz, das Festival von oben herab zu organisieren. "

Hyun Sil Lee, Hausfrau

"Now Citizens Should Take the Initiative."

Six weeks after the end of the festival, the Mayor of Suwon convened around 300 people for a "A Discussion about the Sustainable Implementation of Eco-Mobility," to talk about the EcoMobility Festival follow-up actions. Among the participants were 240 residents from Haenggung-dong, thirteen civil activists, fifteen urban and transport experts, and about thirty interested Suwon citizens. "A round table is the most proper approach towards the realization of direct democracy," Mayor Yeom said with high expectations of the discussion. Two surveys were conducted prior to the round table to identify the main issues to be discussed.

The results of the discussion on the future of Haenggung-dong show that people consider active communication and harmony among residents as the most crucial issue, followed by maintaining and expanding the ecomobile neighborhood over a longer term, and restructuring the local economy.

The round table participants agreed, that a speed limit of twenty kilometers per hour as well as parking controls should be implemented on the two main streets of the quarter. Also, one-way streets are to be introduced. Both streets should become car-free, "thematic streets" every Saturday and Sunday.

Second Vice Mayor Jae-Jun Lee: "While the EcoMobility World Festival project had been driven by the local government followed by the citizens' support, now it's the citizens' turn. Starting from today's discussion, it will be the citizens who take the initiative, while the administration will provide support."

„Jetzt sollen die Bürger initiativ werden. "

Sechs Wochen nach dem Festival lud der Suwoner Bürgermeister rund 300 Bürger zu einem „Gespräch über die nachhaltige Einführung von Ökomobilität" ein, um Folgemaßnahmen nach dem Festival zu diskutieren. Unter den Teilnehmern waren 240 Einwohner von Haenggung-dong, 13 Aktivisten, 15 Stadt- und Verkehrsexperten sowie etwa 30 interessierte Bürger aus dem weiteren Suwon.

„Ein Runder Tisch ist der geeignetste Ansatz, um direkte Demokratie zu verwirklichen", sagte Bürgermeister Yeom mit hohen Erwartungen an die Diskussion. Vorerhebungen halfen, die Hauptanliegen für die Diskussion zu bestimmen.

Die Diskussion über die Zukunft Haenggung-dongs zeigte, dass das Hauptanliegen der Bürger die aktive Kommunikation und Harmonie zwischen den Bewohnern war, gefolgt von der Beibehaltung und Ausweitung des ökomobilen Quartiers über längere Zeit sowie der Restrukturierung der Wirtschaft im Quartier.

Die Versammlung hat sich dafür ausgesprochen, dass auf den zwei Hauptstraßen des Viertels ein Tempolimit von 20 Stundenkilometern gelten sowie eine Parkraumüberwachung eingeführt werden soll. Auch sollen Einbahnstraßen eingerichtet werden. Beide Straßen sollen jeden Samstag und Sonntag autofrei und zu „thematischen Straßen" werden.

Vizebürgermeister Jae-Jun Lee: „Während das Projekt des EcoMobility World Festivals von der Stadtverwaltung betrieben und anschließend von den Bürgern unterstützt worden war, sind jetzt die Bürger dran. Von der heutigen Diskussion ab werden es die Bürger sein, die Initiativen ergreifen, während die Verwaltung diese unterstützen wird."

In March 2014, Suwon City convened the second round-table discussion. Around 500 people gathered at a Suwon gymnasium to discuss Suwon's future transportation plan: hundreds of citizens as well as the Mayor, city councilors, members of parliament, transport experts, bus and taxi drivers, university students, and others.

Using a remote election system, 500 participants' opinions and answers to specific questions on problems and solutions around urban transportation were simultaneously gathered, and immediately and transparently presented on the screen to all of the participants.

Participants identified the growing number of cars, the increase in commuters with insufficient public transport facilities, as well as the incomplete and decrepit road network as main issues.

The encouraging outcome: the expansion of EcoMobility policies was considered the most needed policy to tackle the current and future transportation problems and to meet the citizens' mobility needs. On the other hand, people wanted more public parking spaces.

"All of the voices collected here at the round tables will be actively collected into Suwon's transportation policy," was the promise made by Mayor Yeom.

Im März 2014 organisierte die Stadt Suwon einen zweiten Runden Tisch. Um die 500 Leute versammelten sich in einer Suwoner Sporthalle, um Suwons zukünftigen Verkehrsleitplan zu diskutieren: Hunderte von Bürgern sowie der Bürgermeister, Stadträte, Kongressabgeordnete, Verkehrsexperten, Bus- und Taxifahrer, Universitätsstudenten und andere.

Mit Hilfe eines Fernwahlsystems wurden die Meinungen und Antworten der 500 Teilnehmer auf bestimmte Fragen rund um den Stadtverkehr gesammelt und sofort auf dem Bildschirm gezeigt.

Als Hauptprobleme benannten die Teilnehmer die steigende Zahl von Autos, das Anwachsen der Pendlerzahlen bei unzureichendem öffentlichem Vekehrsangebot sowie das unvollständige und heruntergekommene Straßennetz.

Das ermutigende Resultat: Die Ausweitung des Ökomobilitätsprogramms wurde als dringend notwendige Strategie betrachtet, um die heutigen und künftigen Verkehrsprobleme in den Griff zu bekommen und den Mobilitätsbedürfnissen der Bürger Rechnung zu tragen. Auf der anderen Seite wünschen sich die Bürger mehr öffentlichen Parkraum.

„Alle Stimmen, die wir hier an den Runden Tischen gesammelt haben, werden in die Suwoner Verkehrspolitik einfließen", versprach Bürgermeister Yeom.

66 I wish this area would stay car-free after this month. 99

99 Ich wünschte, dass dieses Gebiet nach diesem Monat autofrei bliebe. 66

66 This experiment should be repeated next year. 99

99 Dieses Experiment sollte im nächsten Jahr wiederholt werden. 66

66 This area should stay car-free after this month. 99

99 Dieses Gebiet sollte nach diesem Monat auto-frei bleiben. 66

66 I would like to live in an eco-mobile city. 99

99 Ich würde gern in einer öko-mobilen Stadt leben. 66

Healing Hug

On March 1, 2014, Haenggung-dong celebrated the first anniversary of the "Declaration of Independence from Cars." Blocking the traffic, a "Healing Hug" event with dancing and games took place on Hwaseomun Street. Mayor Yeom spoke at the high point of the event, which was a hugging and healing moment among the neighbors.

Haenggung-dong residents have been transforming their neighborhood into a place that is safe and relaxed, and where it is possible to live an ecomobile lifestyle. There is no doubt that the EcoMobility World Festival contributed greatly to this. While the festival was a great success, quarrels among the residents occur about the best way to use cars, and this was a major bone of contention during a round-table discussion in November 2013.

Heilende Umarmung

Am 1. März 2014 feierte Haenggung-dong den ersten Jahrestag der „Unabhängigkeitserklärung von Autos". Auf der gesperrten Hwaseomun-Straße fand ein Happening „Heilende Umarmung" mit Gemeinschaftstänzen und Spielen statt. Bürgermeister Yeom sprach bei deren Höhepunkt, einer heilenden Gruppenumarmung der Nachbarn.

Die Bewohner von Haenggung-dong haben das Quartier in einen Ort verwandelt, der sicher und entspannt ist und wo es sich mit einem ökomobilen Lebensstil gut leben lässt – inspiriert durch das EcoMobility World Festival. Während das Festival ein großer Erfolg war, sind die Zerwürfnisse unter den Bewohnern über den Gebrauch von Autos immer noch heftig, wie während des Runden Tisches m November 2013 offenbar wurde.

The Festival's Legacy
Das Vermächtnis des Festivals

Car-free month
Simulation exercise
Sustainable neighborhood
Festival
Model community
Pilot project
Mise-en-scène
Social experiment
Community-building
Green lifestyle
Sustainable transport

Reticence Broken—Social Interaction Spurred

Conceived as a mobility-focused initiative, the festival unfolded an unforeseen effectiveness as a community-building project. Neighbors who reportedly did not talk to each other for fifty years are now chatting and discussing common matters. Whether it was disputes about the removal of cars for a month or excited conversations on better streets and squares—the community of the Haenggung-dong neighborhood emerged revived from the festival.

Renewed Haenggung-dong = Pricier Quarter

Through the festival, Haenggung-dong has become a place where many Suwon people, especially young families with children, would like to live—it's centrally located, fairly quiet, shows a charming ambience and characteristic houses. This is the upside.

The downside is that the market has responded with an increase in real estate prices and rents. Ironically and sadly, a businesswoman who had initially opposed the festival and later become a supporter could not maintain her business in the area, because the rising value of the property made the building owner pursue other more profitable plans.

Cars Returned—Quality of Life Curtailed

Many elderly people have regretted the return of the cars. They had come to appreciate the space for casual meetings and little chats, the safe walking in the streets, and the entertaining games and performances on the squares. "It's a pity," a woman said, "during the past month I grew bell peppers in plant pots in front of my house—now it's no longer possible because the motor traffic is back."

Schweigsamkeit gebrochen – soziale Interaktion beflügelt

Als mobilitätsfokussierte Initiative konzipiert, hat das Festival eine unvorhersehbare Wirksamkeit als gemeinschaftsbildendes Projekt entfaltet. Nachbarn, die laut Berichten über 50 Jahre nicht miteinander gesprochen hatten, halten nun einen Schwatz und diskutieren gemeinsame Anliegen. Ob es Auseinandersetzungen über die Entfernung der Autos für einen Monat oder anregende Unterhaltungen über bessere Straßen und Plätze waren – die Gemeinschaft des Quartiers Haenggung-dong wurde durch das Festival neu belebt.

Erneuertes Haenggung-dong = teureres Quartier

Durch das Festival ist Haenggung-dong ein Ort geworden, an dem viele Suwoner Einwohner, besonders Familien mit Kindern, gern leben würden – es ist zentral gelegen, ziemlich ruhig, bietet ein charmantes Wohnumfeld und charakteristische Häuser.

Der Nachteil ist, dass der Markt darauf mit einem Anstieg der Immobilien- und Mietpreise reagiert hat. Ironischer- und bedauerlicherweise konnte eine Geschäftsfrau, die anfangs gegen das Festival gewesen und später eine Unterstützerin geworden war, ihren Laden im Quartier nicht aufrechterhalten, weil der gestiegene Wert des Grundstücks den Eigentümer dazu veranlasste, eine profitablere Nutzung zu verfolgen.

Autos zurückgekehrt – Lebensqualität beschnitten

Viele ältere Leute haben die Wiederkehr der Autos bedauert. Sie schätzten den Raum für zwanglose Gespräche und Schwätzchen, die sichere Bewegung auf den Straßen und die unterhaltsamen Spiele und Aufführungen auf den Plätzen. „Es ist schade", sagte eine Frau, „während des vergangenen Monats hatte ich in Pflanztöpfen vor meinem Haus Paprika gezogen – jetzt geht das nicht mehr, weil der Autoverkehr zurück ist."

Johannesburg
South Africa
1-31 October

EcoMobility
WorldFestival
2015

Future Festivals Ahead

Inspired by the world's first EcoMobility Festival in Suwon, several cities around the world have been considering organizing the next festivals. Imagine: one month without cars in a city quarter in South Africa, China, Brazil, Taiwan, Tunisia, the United States …

Johannesburg in South Africa prepares to free a business district from motor traffic for a month in cooperation with the companies located there. "We want to close off certain streets in Sandton, our second largest Central Business District (CBD) to car traffic during the entire Transport Month in October 2015", announced the Executive Mayor of the City of Johannesburg, Cllr Parks Tau. "We want to show residents, commuters, and visitors that an ecomobile city is possible and that public transport, walking, and cycling can be accessible, safe, attractive, and cool!" (http://www.ecomobilityfestival.org)

Zukünftige Festivals stehen bevor

Angeregt durch das welterste EcoMobility Festival in Suwon, erwägen mehrere Städte in aller Welt, die nächsten Festivals zu veranstalten. Man stelle sich vor: ein Monat ohne Autos in einem Stadtquartier in Südafrika, China, Brasilien, Taiwan, Tunesien, den Vereinigten Staaten …

Johannesburg in Südafrika schickt sich an, einen Geschäftsbezirk in Zusammenarbeit mit den dort ansässigen Wirtschaftsunternehmen für einen Monat vom Kraftfahrzeugverkehr zu befreien. „Wir wollen während des gesamten Monats Oktober 2015 bestimmte Straßen in Sandton, unserem zweitgrößten Central Business District (CBD), für Autos sperren", kündigte der Johannesburger Bürgermeister Parks Tau an. „Wir wollen den Bewohnern, Pendlern und Besuchern zeigen, dass ein ökomobiler Lebenstil möglich ist und dass öffentlicher Nahverkehr, Gehen und Radfahren für jeden zugänglich, sicher und attraktiv sein können – und eine coole Art der Mobilität!" (http://www.ecomobilityfestival.org)

Acknowledgments
Danksagung

Suwon City Government Tae-young Yeom (Mayor). **Executive Committee:** Jaejoon Lee (Vice-Mayor of Suwon), Jongho-Do, Yonghak Lee, Changseok Han, Gwanjae Lee, Seongho Lee, Youngok Choi, Namkyun Shin, Sangseok Song, Cheolwook Hong, Hyungbok Kim, Gangui Choi, Yeonhee Park, Geonmo Yoon, Heungsoo Park, Bongyoung Choi, Snagseon Bae. Choongyoung Kim. **Planning and Operative Committee:** Choongwan Kim, Minho Roh, Tagyoon Kim, Doyoung Kim. **Officials of Festival Neighborhood:** Geonmo Yoon, Beomseon Lee, Jeongwan Lim. **Executive Bureau:** Heungsoo Park, Byeongik Kim, Yeonjoo Hwang, Jangyoung Lee, Doyong Gwak, Soongee Seo, Hakseo Lee, Namhee Koo, Insu Jang, Soohyang Kim, Hyunjung Ko, Inkyu Song, Jiyoung Kim, Ohsun Yang, Jeongsook Dong, Daesup Kim, Jongsup Lee, Hoon Kim, Joongrok Ahn, Sangmyoung Lee, Gyeongah Ko, Youngran Roh, Heeran Joo, Gyounghyo Yoon, Gyounghwa Park. **Admistrative Supporters:** Hyunsook Lee, Gapseong Park, Namcheol Cho, Sunkyoung Kim, Hyoungoo Roh, Jeongman Shim, Seonjae Lee, Sangwoo Kim, Jaejoon Lee, Jaewoo Ahn, Hyeonsook Park. Byeongpo Lim, Hyogeun Min, Wooyeol Lee, Hasoo Kim, Jeonghee Kwon, Cheolho Wang, Seongyong Shin, Seoktaek Han, Sangyoo Choi, Hyeongoo Lee, Gyusook Shim, Sangtae Kim, Hongshik Yoon, Jonghwa Lee, Hyunjoo Choi, Youngjin Hyun, Deuksoon Park, Gyoosung Lee, Sanghee Lee, Doyoung Lee, Woonoh Baek, Youngran Kim, Bongsoo Jeong, Inbo Shim, Choonghyun Baek, Haengsoon Park, Younghwan Oh, Myungsoon Moon, Manho Roh, Youngeun Lee, Yongoo Woo, Younghoon Lee. **ICLEI World Secretariat:** Konrad Otto-Zimmermann, Santosh Kodukula, Sophie Verstraelen, Jiwon Lee, Eilish O'Loughlin, Mona Ludigkeit, Marta dal Lago, Katrina Borromeo, Monika Zimmermann. Korea Office: Yeonhee Park, Goowon Kim, Youngmee Choi, Hyunmin Shim, Elly Lee, Jeongmuk Kang, Matic Kin, Minjin Lee, Taesun Yu, Sugum Han. **THE URBAN IDEA** Konrad Otto-Zimmermann, Jan Zederbohm, Mareike Schalberger, Kornelia Zimmermann, Theresa Zimmermann. **UN-HABITAT** André Dzikus, Kulwant Singh. **Documentalists Fietscher Film:** Daniel Huhn. **TU Berlin:** Tobias Kuttler. **Residents, Citizens and Civil Society Neighborhood Office:** Gyoengah Ko, Duksoon Lim, Gyeonghee Han, Gyeongah Lee, Insun Lim, Jinsook Sung. **EcoMobility Village Storytellers:** Youngae Kwon, Gyoungja Kim, Geummi Kim, Sungchae Kim, Okjin Kim 1, Okjin Kim 2, Hyungsoo Kim, Geumok Sul, Jungha Oh, Sungjin Yoon, Myoungsook Lee 1, Myoungsook Lee 2, Yongsun Lee, Jonglim Lee, Pansoo Lee, Hyesook Lee, Hyeyoung Lee, Byoungkwan Cho, Sookhee choi, Insook Choi, Jongwoon Choi, Hangryul Choi, Minsook Hwang, Seunguk Lee, Youngsook Lee, Youngmi Lee. **Velotaxi drivers:** Joon Han, Jungsun Jeong, Miri Hwang, Youngae Park, Youngkwan Oh, Eulryong Han, Jeongsook Ko, Seoungryong Lee. **EcoMobility Community Dancing Crew NILRIRI:** Kirayng Kwon, Myoungsook Kim, Myoungja Kim, Youngsook Kim, Joongbae Kim, Choonhwan Kim, Geumsung No, Joongja Park, Jinsook Seong, Gwangboon Lee, Youngsook Lee, Yongsoon Lee, Oksoon Lee, Okja Lee, Jungja Lee, Hyeyoung Lee, Hosoon Lee, Hwasoon Lee, Duksoon Lim, Ansoon Lim, Youngja Lim, Insung Lim, Younghee Jeong, Jungsun Jeong, Soonrok Cho, Hoosook Choo, Insoon Cha, Myoungwoon Choi, Younghee Choi, Miri Hwan. **Local Surveyors:** Geungja Kong, Kija Kwong,

Yeonja Ki, Youngsook Kim, Younghee Kim, Jeongmi Kim, Park, Hyekyoung Park, Soonduk Paek, Youngsook Lee, Soonkoo Jeong, Youngja Chae. **EcoMobility Travel Supporters** Koo, Nakkyun Kim, Sangho Kim, Sukwoo Kim, Youngkyu Kim, Kilhan Yoon, Bonghyeon Yoon, Sooknchul Yoon, Kangwook Lee, Jeong, Byoungkwan Cho, Jongwoon Choi, Hangryul Choi. Kim, Sahyun Kim, Eunpyo Kim, Changyeop Kim, Taehyung Kim, Park, Gunhee Peak, Minji Seo, Gyoungwon Son, Sinsil Song, Dohyon Lee, Yoobin Lee, Jaemin Lee, Hyunjoo Lee, Sohee Sookwon Jeong, Hanul Jeong, Soohyun Cho, Inhye Choo, **Youth Supporters:** Hyuntae Huh (Researcher, Suwon Research Hochul Park (Director, Hangkoong-Dong Culture Super), **Supporters:** Haeun Kil, Dongin Kim, Yeonchang Kim, Joonkyu Park, Seungeun Oh, Jeonghyun Oh, Changhoon Yoon, Dayoung Chooyoung Park, Chaeyoung Sin, Soobin Jeon, Soobin Kang, Kim, Heesun No, Nani Park, Sooyeong Park, Jieun Park,

Joongbae Kim, Hyeongsoo Kim, Sooyong Moon, Youngae Yoonwoo Lee, Hyejin Lee, Insun Lim, Gyoungsook Jeong, **/ Sangrok Volunteers:** Youngman Kang, Hanin Kwak, Hyunhoi Ilkwon Kim, Gwangnam Ahn, MyoungkyunAhn, Jaejoon Yeom, Dukjin Lee, Yongsun Lee, Jonglim Lee, Jaehoo Jeong, Jinyang **Youth Journalists:** Chaeyoung Kwon, Goochan Kim, Soojin Haeun Kim, Seri Min, Sangeun Park, Jeyoung Park, Jiyoung Hwanho Yoo, Yekyum Yoon, Gyoungmi Lee, Gyoungyeb Lee, Lim, Jinjoo Lim, Yeaji Jeon, Hyebin Jeon, Gyoungmin Chung, Bumsoo Choi, Hyunchae Choi, Jungwon Huh. **Helpers for** Institute) Heysook Song (Hangkoong-Dong Residency Artist), Hyoungsoo Kim (Suwon KYC Hwasung Kilajobi). **Youth** Kim, Gwangeun Park, Minsuk Park, Sangmin Park, Jihyung Lee, Hojoon Chung, Changyeob Kim, Taehyung Kim, Yeaji Park, Yoomin Kang, Daeun Kim, Wooeun Kim, Jughyun Kim, Jiyeon Hyehyun Park, Gyunhoo Yang, Hyejin Yum, Hyewon Oh, Eunhye

Yoo, Donghyung Lee, Jungin Lee, Eunjii Lim, Soyoun Chang, Hanul Jeong, Soojin Cho 1, Soojin Cho 2, Eun jin Choi, Hyunji Choi, Heesun Choi, Jisoo Koo, Dabin Kim, Minjook Kim, Minkyu Kim, Bomin Kim, Jiwon Par, Sooji Ahn, Yoosub Yoon, Donghee Lee, Soojeong Lee, Eunji Choi, Insoo Choi, Sungmin Kim, Yein Kim, Yookyoung Kim, Jeesoo Kim, Jeeyoon Kim, Chaerin Kim, Taehui Kim, Minchoo Park, Jihyun Park, Hyunji Pae, Sungjoo Byun, Yejin Son, JAhyun Son, Jahyun Song, Yookyoung Sin, Dabin Lee, Sohyun Lee, Soyoun Lim, Eunbi Chang, Soobin Jeong, Hayeon Chung, Uijeong Choi, Seoyoung Kim, Yejin Kim, Heyeok Kim, Yoojin No, Hanhee Park, Sinsil Song, Boyoung Yoon, Jiho Lee, Sungmin Jeon, Hyebin Jeon, Yeonjin Choi, Ryunhoi Song, Sukyoung Song, Jungnim Yoo, Mihwa Lim, Ahyun Lee, Yeji Cho, Minjoo Kim, Soojin Kim, Jiyeon Kim, Seoyoung No, Hyerim No, Sookyoung Park, Hanul Park, Hansol Pae, Chaerin Song, Eunji Yang, Eunjin Yang, Soobin Oh, Jaeyoon Yoo, Dohyun Lee, Minsung Lee, Ahyun Lee, Youngah Lee, Jooeun Lee, Yeji Jeon, Soohyun Cho, Inhye Choo, Jieun Cha, Jungin Choi, Heejin Choi, Sulki Han, Jeongmin Hwang, Dahee Kim, Kibum Park, Sehwan Park, Hyunil Lim, Youngsuk Chang, Gyoungsuk Joo, Munseon Jin, Jeongeun Choi, Choonghyun Han, Jisoo Hong, Yongsuk Koo, Dongjoon Kim, Bosuk Kim, Jongyoon Kim, Jiyeon Kim, Jinha Kim, Pooreum Kim, Yoojeong Namkoong, Dasom Park, Uijae Paek, Dongin Seo, Siyoung Song, Eunseon Song, Daehae Ui, Minkyu Lee, Soomin Lee, Choongsoo Lee, Sunchoon Kim, Sunjoon Kim Joonyoung Ha. **Family volunteer group of Maehyang Middle School: Students:** Seonho Choi, Hyunjeong Kim, Taehoon Kim, Jisoo Kim, Yoorim Jeon, Gyoungkeun Cho, Jooeun Lee, Hyunwoo Oh, Youngjoon Kim, Jiwoo Jwon, Sola Lee, Minhee Son, Sangeun Hong, Jangjoon Seo, Dasom Park, Changrok Lee, Jimin Kim, Jonghyuk Park, Yoonki Hong, Seongeun Lee, Sohee Cho, Jaehyuk Park, Changhyun Kim, Jihyun Song, Soojin No, Sunjoon Kim., Gyukwa Choi, Jihwan Kwon, Sooin Choo, Heesoo Oh, Heyjin Kim, Yejin Song, Yeonsoo Jeon, Wonmyoung Yeom, Hyunsoo Kim, Yeaeun Jeong, Hyein Kim, Jiyoun Kim, Sangah Park, Rina Jang, Wonho Lee, Seongjoo Yeon, Yea bin Lim, Jimyoung Han. **Parents:** Younghee Jin, Youngran Lee, Misun Han, Gyoungran Lim, Moonhee Choi, Hyunjeong Jeong, Jooyoung Lee, Hyangwok Park, Gyoungsook Choo, Younghee Kim, Eunyoung Sul, Heysoon Lee, Hyunsook Kook, Youngyeh Park, Yoonsook Park, Hyesook Choi, Gyoungah Lee, Jungja Lee, Leehwa Cho, Younghee Kim, Jeongmi Yook, Gyoungok Lee, Jungkyu Choi, Young Jin, Seongjong Lee, Jungsuk Yeon, Junghwa Han. **University Students Supporters:** Sooyoun Kwak, Bomin Kim, Ayoung Kim, Taeyoon Kim, Jeongmin Nam, Byoungho Park, Jooyoung Park, Hyunjoo Park, Yoonah Song, Jaeun Sim, Uiyeon Won, Moonsuk Choi, Changho Seon, Chaeyeon Lim, Yeonjung Yoon, Minhye Yang, Taeyang Lee, Hana Lee, Seongwon Cha, Jaeyong Choi, Bomnal Han, Soojeong Hong, Daeyoung Kwon, Chorok Park, Choyeon Park, Sooin Seo, Seonghee Yoo, Yoonsub Lee, Jeongeun Lim, Myoungjoo Jeong, Gyoungmin Kim, Gyoungtae Kim, Choa Park. **Traditional Play Teams:** Nambook Lee, Chilbosan Dotori Gyosil Pulmuedle. **Cultural Activity Organizing Team:** Hyesook Song, Hocheol Park, Eunju Song, Moonhee Han, Jeomkyun Oh, Youngram Roh, Seungjun Ryu, Soook Noh, Seongho Yoon, Seonhoon Lee, Soolin Yoon, Bitna Lee, Sein Oh, Wonkyoung Lee, Donghee Kim, Sekyoung Choi, Barasi Han, Younghwan Jang, Seonmi Lee, Minjeong Kim. **Companies and Associations:** Community Dance Aha, Alternative Space Noon, Photographers recording Suwon, Seed Gallery, Hanggungjae, Korea Artists Association Suwon Branch, Hanggung Youth Group, Hanggungdong Community Art Center. **Haenggung-dong Residents' Group:** 1,280 members.

SUWON City
South Korea
1–30 September
EcoMobility
WorldFestival
2013

Festival Makers
Festivalveranstalter

Organizers Organisatoren
Suwon City, ICLEI
Creative Director Kreativdirektor
Konrad Otto-Zimmermann
Presenters Veranstalter
ICLEI, UN-HABITAT
Ambassadors Botschafter
Gil Peñalosa, Boyoung Park, Chul Park
International Advisors Internationale Berater
Florian Lennert, Gil Peñalosa

Picture Credits
Bildnachweis

ICLEI: 77 ▶, 83 ◥, 83 ◢; (Jeongho Lee, Hwasu Shin): 9, 10, 16 ▲, 16 ◣, 17, 21 ▲, 27 ◢, 28 ◥, 28 ◢, 29 ◣, 29 ◢, 30, 31 ◥, 37, 39, 40, 41 ◀, 41 ◥, 43 ▶, 43 ◣, 44 ◥, 45 ▶, 45 ◥, 46, 47 ◢, 48, 50 ▶, 50 ▶, 53 ◣, 53 ◢, 55 ◢, 58, 59 ▶, 59 ◣, 59 ▼, 59 ◢, 60 ◢, 61 ◣, 61 ◢, 62 ◢, 63 ◢, 64, 66 ▼, 66 ◢, 67, 68 ▶, 68 ◀, 68 ◣, 69, 70, 71, 72, 73 ◥, 74 ◢, 80 ◥, 84, 85, 86 ▶, 86 ◀, 86 ◣, 86 ▼, 87 ◥, 88, 89, 90, 92, 94, 95, 96, 97 ◣, 97 ▼, 97 ◢, 98 ▶, 98 ◣; (Sophie Verstraelen): 22, 29 ◣, 62 ◣,
Suwon City (Kisoo Kim, Byunghoon Sul et.al.): 7, 12 ▶, 13, 14 ▲, 14 ▼, 15 ◀, 15 ▶, 19 ▼, 24-25, 33 ◥, 45 ◢, 47 ◥, 47 ▶, 52, 56, 63 ▶, 63 ◥, 66 ◣, 77 ◀, 81 ◥, 81 ◢, 87 ◢, 93 ◣, 98 ◀, 98 ◥, 104, 105, 107,
The Urban Idea (Konrad Otto-Zimmermann): 8 ▼, 11 ◀, 18, 20 ▶, 20 ◀, 20 ◣, 21 ◀, 21 ◣, 21 ▶, 21 ◢, 27 ▶, 31 ◀, 32, 34, 35, 36 ▼, 44 ▶, 45 ◣, 49, 50 ◣, 51, 55 ◥, 57 ◥, 60 ◣, 65, 66 ▲, 68 ◣, 73 ▶, 74 ◣, 76, 78, 79, 82 ◥, 83 ▶, 83 ◀, 83 ◣, 100, 101, 109 ▶, 109 ◣,
Changwon City: 12 ◀
Johannesburg City: 109 ◥
Kilian Kreiser: Infografiken Information diagrams 19, 26, 41, 80, 81, 87, 93
Tobias Kuttler: 8 ◀, 54, 61 ▲, 62 ▲, 75, 91, 102, 103, 106
Seoul City: 16 ◢
Jeonghyeon Song: 36 ▲
Theresa Zimmermann: 28 ◣, 57 ▶, 57 ▲, 59 ◥, 60 ▲, 63 ◣, 82 ◣, 86 ◢, 97 ▲, 99

Imprint
Impressum

© 2015 by jovis Verlag GmbH
Texts by kind permission of the authors.
Pictures by kind permission of the photographers/holders of the picture rights.
Das Copyright für die Texte liegt bei den Autoren.
Das Copyright für die Abbildungen liegt bei den Fotografen/Inhabern der Bildrechte.
All rights reserved.
Alle Rechte vorbehalten.

Cover Umschlagmotiv: Jeongho Lee
Editors and Authors Herausgeber und Autoren: Konrad Otto-Zimmermann, Yeonhee Park
Co-author Mitautor: Tobias Kuttler
With contributions by Mit Beiträgen von: Katrina Borromeo, Jeongmuk Kang, Santhosh Kodukula, Hye-Jung Lee, Mona Ludigkeit, Sophie Verstraelen, Theresa Zimmermann
Photographs Fotografien: Kisoo Kim, Santhosh Kodukula, Tobias Kuttler, Jeonghoo Lee, Konrad Otto-Zimmermann, Hwasu Shin, Byunghoon Sul, Sophie Verstraelen, Theresa Zimmermann
Infographics Infografiken: Kilian Kreiser
Proofreading English Korrektur Englisch: Inez Templeton, Ciara Leonhard
Lithography Lithografie: Bild1Druck, Berlin
Setting Satz: jovis Verlag: Vanessa Wodrich, Yvonne Illig
Printing and binding Druck und Bindung: Graspo CZ a.s., Zlín
Bibliographic information published by the Deutsche Nationalbibliothek
The Deutsche Nationalbibliothek lists this publication in the Deutsche Nationalbibliografie; detailed bibliographic data are available on the Internet at http://dnb.d-nb.de
Bibliografische Information der Deutschen Nationalbibliothek
Die Deutsche Nationalbibliothek verzeichnet diese Publikation in der Deutschen Nationalbibliografie; detaillierte bibliografische Daten sind im Internet über http://dnb.d-nb.de abrufbar.

jovis Verlag GmbH
Kurfürstenstraße 15/16
10785 Berlin

www.jovis.de

jovis books are available worldwide in selected bookstores. Please contact your nearest bookseller or visit www.jovis.de for information concerning your local distribution.
jovis-Bücher sind weltweit im ausgewählten Buchhandel erhältlich. Informationen zu unserem internationalen Vertrieb erhalten Sie von Ihrem Buchhändler oder unter www.jovis.de.

ISBN 978-3-86859-294-8

The Partners
Die Partner

Suwon, a city of 1.2 million inhabitants near South Korea's capital city Seoul, hosted the EcoMobility World Festival 2013. Suwon City was recognized as a finalist for

the 2014 Sustainable Transport Award, which recognizes its innovative and sustainable transportation project that improves mobility conditions for the residents, reduces greenhouse gas emissions and air pollution, and improves safety and access for cyclists and pedestrians. In addition, the participatory process and lifestyle shift was recognized. Suwon City was also awarded the 2014 UN-HABITAT Scroll of Honour for its citizen-initiated governance and participatory urban planning and budgeting approach at neighborhood and broader city level.

Suwon, eine Stadt von 1,2 Millionen Einwohnern nahe der südkoreanischen Hauptstadt Seoul, veranstaltete das EcoMobility World Festival 2013.

Die Stadt Suwon wurde als „Finalist" (Stadt in der engeren Wahl) für den Sustainable Transport Award 2014 für ihr innovatives und nachhaltiges Verkehrsprojekt ausgezeichnet, welches die Mobilitätsbedingungen für die Einwohner verbessert, verkehrsbedingte Treibhausgasemissionen und Luftverschmutzung verringert sowie die Sicherheit und Durchlässigkeit für Radfahrer und Fußgänger erhöht hat. Zusätzlich wurden der intensive Beteiligungsprozess und die Veränderung des Lebensstils anerkannt.

Die Stadt Suwon wurde auch mit der UN-HABITAT Scroll of Honour für seine partizipative Stadt- und Haushaltsplanung auf Quartiers- wie gesamtstädtischer Ebene ausgezeichnet.

UN-HABITAT — www.unhabitat.org

UN-Habitat is the United Nations program working towards a better urban future. To help address the mobility challenge, UN-Habitat offers a comprehensive package of knowledge, advocacy, and technical assistance to support national governments and local authorities in the development and implementation of sustainable urban mobility plans and investment strategies.

UN-Habitat ist das UN-Programm, das an einer besseren städtischen Zukunft arbeitet. Um der Herausforderung „Mobilität" zu begegnen, bietet UN-Habitat ein umfassendes Paket von Wissen, Interessensvertretung und fachlicher Hilfe an, um Regierungen und Kommunen bei der Entwicklung und Umsetzung nachhaltiger Stadtverkehrs- und Investitionspläne zu unterstützen.

ICLEI — www.iclei.org

ICLEI is the world's leading association of cities and local governments dedicated to sustainable development. It is a powerful movement of twelve megacities, one hundred supercities and urban regions, 450 large cities, as well as 450 medium-sized cities and towns in 86 countries. ICLEI's EcoMobility program—a global campaign on sustainable urban transport—aims to promote the use of more public and non-motorized transportation, enhance the efficiency of vehicles, and use urban planning to improve transportation systems.

ICLEI ist der führende Weltverband von Städten und Kommunen, die sich nachhaltiger Entwicklung verschrieben haben. Er ist eine starke Bewegung von 12 Megastädten, 100 Superstädten und Stadtregionen, 450 Großstädten sowie 450 Mittel- und Kleinstädten in 86 Ländern. ICLEIs EcoMobility-Programm, eine weltweite Kampagne zu nachhaltigem Stadtverkehr, will die Nutzung des Umweltverbunds fördern, die Effizienz von Fahrzeugen erhöhen und die Verkehrssysteme auch über die Stadtplanung verbessern.

The Urban Idea — www.theurbanidea.com

The Urban Idea is a couple of creative studios aiming to improve cities through creative concepts and innovative projects. The Urban Idea promotes EcoMobility as a new paradigm of urban mobility and urban transport planning. The studio applies the CityScene methodology to the promotion of EcoMobility by showcasing future sustainable urban mobility in a real city, with real people, in real time. The Creative Director leads the series of EcoMobility World Festivals.

The Urban Idea besteht aus kreativen Studios, die daran arbeiten, Städte durch kreative Konzepte und innovative Projekte zu verbessern. The Urban Idea wirbt für EcoMobility als neues Paradigma der städtischen Mobilität und Verkehrsplanung. Dabei wendet das Studio die CityScene-Methode an, indem zukünftige städtische Mobilität in einer echten Stadt, mit echten Bewohnern in Echtzeit vorgeführt wird. Der Kreativdirektor leitet die Serie von EcoMobility-World-Festivals.